Also by Linda Davies

Self-help:

What Every Woman Needs to Know to Create Financial Abundance

10 Things Everyone Needs to Know About Money

Memoir:

Kidnapped: The true story of my captivity in Iran

Thrillers:

Nest of Vipers

Wilderness of Mirrors

Something Wild

Into the Fire

Final Settlement

Ark Storm

Karma, bloodlines and unfinished business:

Longbow Girl

Gelert's Ghost

Fantasy: The Djinn Quartet:

Sea Djinn

Fire Djinn

Storm Djinn

King of the Djinn

To find out about Linda's latest books and news, please visit www.lindadavies.com

I dedicate this book to:

Yvonne Thomas, honorary aunt and journalist - the woman who, as well as impressing and inspiring my five year-old self, taught me that you can make a career out of words.

And to my niece, Eleanor Beaton, who took and carries the beacon so beautifully for women's empowerment around the world today.

Contents

.

Introduction

My intention with this book is to help women create a healthier relationship with money. The getting. The spending. The borrowing. The saving. The investing. The aim is for women, for YOU, to feel calm, confident and in control. To feel empowered. What I'm offering here will improve both your net worth and your self worth, enabling you to create the abundant financial future of your choice. Of your dreams.

How do we get there?

I offer practical hacks: What to do, how to do it and what not to do. I combine this with psychological tools and insights to guide you. Only when we understand our deep inner, psychological relationship with money can we begin to make decisions that are free of the old and powerful conditioning that all too often holds us back.

To start off, I look to see how men are doing. At the multiple money gaps that exist. Why? Because if we identify them, and look at why they exist, we can better reduce them. The gaps show what is possible for us. But I want to do more than catch up. I want you to create what is optimum, liberating and most abundant for you.

So let's look at those gaps.

The gender pay gap continues, as does the gender pensions chasm. There are gaps in how women spend and invest relative to men, in how we teach our girls and boys about money and their place in the world. There are disparities in our attitudes to money and how we operate in the financial sphere. There are radical differences in the way the money world speaks to us. Or doesn't. There is an aspiration gap, born of differential conditioning, entitlement and ambition. Our relationship with debt is different from that of men. We pay more than men to obtain debt. We get the worst kinds pushed on us and have less access to the good kinds. And to cap it all, we are more likely to suffer economic and financial abuse than men which renders us particularly vulnerable to the domestic violence that typically goes hand-in-hand with such abuse.

All of this does huge, cumulative damage to our financial literacy, and our financial health. Past, present and future.

All of this exists in a context of rising prices.

My aim is to help women begin to close these gaps today, and to increase our financial health and resilience by improving our knowledge of the money world and our own money psychology, both conscious, and unconscious.

The role of psychology is enormous. The attitudes of our parents and our grandparents, how we were raised, the views of our friends, our social and work cohort, determine our relationship with money. Sometimes healthy. Often not.

These belief systems can be hardwired into our brain so deeply we don't even know they're there. Yet they pull our financial strings, these silent puppet masters, holding us back, damaging our financial health.

I will share these key deep-seated beliefs so that we might recognise them in ourselves. I will give you tools to unearth them, and turn them into a healthier money psychology that can transform our financial and general health.

I will also share how and where we are manipulated psychologically by the corporate world so that we can recognise that and fight back.

If we understand why we behave as we do, what exactly our money psychology looks like, if we can recognise external manipulation then we are far more able to counteract this and implement the practical "how to" aspects of this book. These practical tips and suggestions will work together to help us spend mindfully, save more and invest better.

All of this will help us create the abundant financial future of our dreams.

Let's get started.

Chapter One: The gender pay gap - still going strong

Why?

What can we do about it?

- Globally, the average woman's annual income is $11,000, just under half what the average man earns – $21,000.[1]

- These averages conceal shocking extremes between and across genders. Over 90% of Cocoa Farmers in the Côte d'Ivoire are paid less than half what the World Bank believes is a "living income" ($2.50 a day[2]). The situation for women is even worse. The African Development Bank estimates that women perform 68% of the labour involved in cocoa production but earn just 21% of the income generated.[3]

- The World Economic Forum predicts it will take 257 years to close the workplace gap at the current rate of progress.[4]

- Sheryl Sandberg, the former COO of Facebook argues that "38% of the pay gap… is bias… It is gender… There is no other explanation."[5]

- In the UK in 2021, the gender pay gap among all employees was 15.4%.[6]

- In the US, the average woman earned only 82% of the average man's earnings[7] - to make up the difference she'd need to work an additional *39 days a year*.

- Black women would have to work an extra 233 days to make up the difference.

- Mothers would have to work an extra 161 days[8] each year to counteract the motherhood penalty, earning $406,280 less over a 40 year career.

- Transgender women's average earnings fall by nearly one-third after transition.[9]

- Gargantuan pay gaps exist in the sporting world with male prize winners typically receiving multiple times what female winners receive.

One of the most fundamental ways in which we can improve our financial health is to earn more. The stats above tell us we are earning *less*. Welcome to the gender pay gap.

The context

I'm going to analyse this gap in some detail because understanding its different components is crucial if we are going to tackle these as individuals and as a society.

You might think that progress in the legal equality framework would be reducing the gender pay gap and other associated gaps, particularly if we look at developed economies such as the United Kingdom and United States. What emerges is a strange stubbornness, an invisible brake that holds women back from gender pay equality.

Historical note: The stubborn persistence of female poverty

Writer Louise Ericsson offers a fascinating but disturbing historical perspective in her *Women and Property in Early Modern England*[10]:

"In the 20th century all our legal restrictions have been removed and yet women as a group remain at a profound economic, social and political disadvantage. Women today predominate amongst those receiving income support or welfare from the state – at the identical rate that they predominated in the 17th century among those in receipt of Parish Poor Relief. And an equivalent proportion of the poor then and now are single mothers. Women today earn only about 2/3 of what men earn and women have earned approximately 2/3 of men's wages for the last seven centuries."

Ericsson asks the $10 million question: *"How is it that such severe economic disparity between women and men persists when the laws have changed so dramatically?"*

Has the picture improved? Have the ensuing decades brought us to the Promised Land?

Debunking the myth of the promised land

Lots of people will tell you *yes*, the picture is rosy. Look at how far you've come. I can't help feeling that the implication here seems to be *we've come far enough* and *we should be satisfied* and *not grumble*, that if we speak up we're *making a fuss about nothing*. This is an argument levelled against women particularly in first world countries. The *what have you got to complain about?* argument.

I'm going to debunk that argument and silence those voices.

I was part of that second wave of feminism, of women who broke down barriers and gained entry to hitherto male-only occupations such as, in my case, investment banking. Having achieved that, I thought the battle was almost over. How wrong was I.

I'm beyond grateful to the *Me Too* movement that has called time on practices in the workplace that I lived with, that many other women and I just took for granted and put up with. The almost daily harassment that just went with the territory. The slights, setbacks and obstacles that were so ubiquitous we never questioned them, maybe didn't even fully see them at the time.

This brave new generation of women have challenged that, changing workplaces, and life, for the better.

But many other changes need to be made as I will address throughout the rest of this book.

Let's start with the gender wage gap in all its facets.

If we look at the workplace from a global perspective, a report from the World Economic Forum in December 2019 predicted depressingly that it would take 257 years to close the workplace gap at the current rate of progress. The same report revealed that globally, the average woman's annual income is $11,500, just under half what the average man earns – $21,500.

Let's break down this gap into different components.

There are three main measures of gaps in pay, earnings and conditions that are typically analysed.

1. *The pay gap* between what the average woman who works earns and what the average man who works earns.
2. *The equivalent earnings gap.* This compares the gap between what men and women doing the same job receive.
3. *The workplace gap.* This measures wage equality, seniority and participation in the labour force.

Average pay gaps around the world

Average pay gaps between the genders vary enormously across countries. If we look at the distance from gender parity in 2016 by region we see in in the Middle East and North Africa it was 39%, in South Asia 33%, East Asia and the Pacific 32%, sub-Saharan Africa 32%, Latin America and the Caribbean 30%, Eastern Europe and central Asia 30%, North America 28%, and in Western Europe, largely thanks to the Scandinavian countries, it was 25%.[11]

If we zoom in a bit more we can find all sorts of other gender pay gaps that vary with the level of overall earnings i.e. the highest earning occupations down to the lowest, and by ethnicity.

Let's have a look in the United Kingdom at the statistics provided by the Office for National Statistics reporting in October 2022.[12] Their report shows that in 2022, the gender pay gap among all employees was 14.9%, a small decrease from the 15.1% gap in 2021, but a larger decrease from 2019's gap of 17.4%. This is still below the gap of 9.0% before the coronavirus pandemic in 2019. Estimates for 2020 and 2021 are subject to more uncertainty than usual therefore we recommend looking at the longer-term trend.

If you exclude part-time employees and focus on full-time employees, the gender pay gap in 2022 actually increased to 8.3%, up from 7.7% in 2021. [In 2020, it was 7.4% down from 9% in April 2019.]

It's worth noting at this point a massive wrinkle in the workforce which does partially but not wholly explain the difference in these figures - a much higher percentage of women work part-time than men. Correspondingly their annual earnings will be lower and this drags down the overall average earnings for women as a whole. Add to this the fact that women are more likely to work in lower paid jobs than men and more of the gap gets explained. But not all, as we shall explore later.

The colour of money - ethnic pay gaps

A report commissioned by The Fawcett Society gives insight into the gender pay gap by ethnicity in Britain.[13]

The chart below shows the full time pay gap between women of different ethnicity and white British men. For white British women, the gap is just under 15%, for black African women it is 20%, for black Caribbean women it is 5%, for Chinese women it is a -6% meaning that Chinese women earn more on average than Chinese men. For Indian women the pay gap is just below 7%, for Pakistani and Bangladeshi women it widens to 18%. For white Irish women the pay gap is a whopping -17%, which shows that white Irish women are out-earning white British men. With regard to white other ethnicities, the pay gap is 14%.

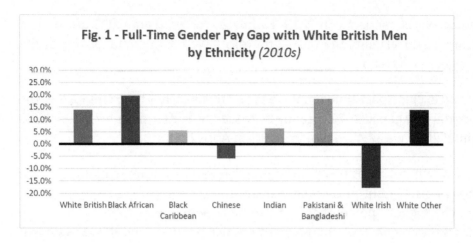

Source: Anthony Breach & Prof. Yaojun Li, The Fawcett Society, *Gender Pay Gap by Ethnicity in Britain - Briefing*, **2017**[14]

Data show that the gender pay gap is narrowing over time but at very different rates. The government has stated that closing the gender pay gap is a priority but they need to ensure that women across different ethnicities within Britain see that their gender pay gap is closed.

The age and level of earnings dimension

If we go back to the Office for National Statistics report of October 2022 we notice another fascinating wrinkle – age.

The report notes: "There remains a large difference in the gender pay gap between employees aged over 40 years and those aged below 40 years."

There's also differentiation according to income level, with the gaps increasing in size for higher earners. The report notes that: "Compared with lower-paid employees, higher earners experience a much larger difference in hourly pay between the sexes. The managers, directors and senior officials' occupation group has experienced the largest fall in gender pay gap since the pre-coronavirus pandemic April 2019 figure, especially for those aged 50 and over; this group has previously been identified as having a notable impact on the pay gap."

There is also a geographic wrinkle. The gender pay gap is higher in every

English region than in Scotland and Northern Ireland.

The United States angle: the equivalent earnings gaps

Data for the United States reported by the organisation PayScale[15] shows that "when men and women with the same employment characteristics do similar jobs, women now earn $0.99 for every dollar that men earn."

That's heartening news but as PayScale themselves note:

"The gap should be zero. It's not zero. In other words, women who are doing the same job as a man, with the exact same qualifications as a man, are still paid one percent less than men at the median for no attributable reason."

But this data hides a wide variety of disparities between occupations. Claudia Goldin in her book *Career and Family*[16] notes that women in tech earn 94 cents on the male tech dollar but women in finance only earn 77 cents on the male finance dollar.

The average pay gap is huge

The Pew Research Center[17] reported that in 2020, on average, looking at full and part-time workers, women earned 84% of what men did. They estimate that this means "it would take an extra 42 days of work for women to earn what men did."

The National Women's Law Center has a nifty chart[18] which shows what closing the pay gap would mean to the average woman:

Two months' supply of groceries	$1,354
Three months' child care payments	$2,778
Three months' rent	$3,213.00

Three months' health insurance premiums	$1,431
Four months' student loan payments	$1,088
Six tanks of gas	$274
Wage gap yearly total:	**$10,157**

When you express the gap in terms of the extra time women would need to work to close it, and of what it costs in terms of monthly standard of living, we see just how iniquitous it is. And this cannot be fully explained by the greater propensity of women to work part time. 25% of women in the Pew Research Center survey said they earned less than a man doing the equivalent job whereas just 5% of men said they earned less than a woman doing the equivalent job. As in the UK, the researchers found that the gap was smaller for younger women than for older. Women in the 25 to 34 age group earned $0.93 for every dollar that a man in the same group earned. To put this in historical context they note that in 1980, women aged 25 to 34 earned 33 cents less than their male counterparts, compared with 7 cents in 2020. The estimated 16-cent gender pay gap among all workers in 2020 was down from 36 cents in 1980.

Gaps, equal pay day, working for nothing and ethnicity gaps

In the US, the American Association of University Women's Equal Pay Day Calendar[19] reveals that March 15 is Equal Pay Day.

This symbolises how far into the year women would need to work to be paid what men received the previous year.[20] To reflect how the pay gap varies between communities, other Equal Pay Days have been added to the calendar. This reveals that many women must work far longer into the year to catch up to men.

- Asian American, Native Hawaiian and Pacific Islander Women's Equal Pay Day is May 3. Asian American and Pacific Islander women are paid 75 cents for every dollar paid to white men
- LGBTQIA+ Equal Pay Awareness Day is June 15
- Moms' Equal Pay Day is September 8. Moms are paid 58 cents for every dollar paid to dads
- Black Women's Equal Pay Day is September 21. Black women are paid 58 cents for every dollar paid to white men
- Latina's Equal Pay Day is December 8. Latinas are paid 54 cents for every dollar paid to white men

Equal Pay Day, UK

In the UK, research from the Fawcett Society[21], calculated on a different basis to that above, shows when the average woman will effectively start working for free. For 2021 this fell on Thursday 18th November.

In the United Kingdom it's very difficult to obtain data for the equivalent earnings gap. This data gap is unhelpful. But some research by consultants, Korn Ferry, published by The Economist in 2017 comparing Britain, France and Germany, is reproduced below.

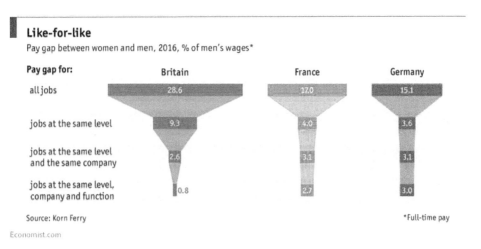

This is encouraging but bearing in mind it is illegal to pay men and women differently for the exact same job it's not surprising that we see this gap diminishing within companies where direct comparison is easier.

However, between companies where there is less visibility of gaps, the results are not so encouraging, particularly in the UK.

And when it comes to averaging out across all jobs, the gap once again becomes huge.

There are those who argue that the average pay gap is unrepresentative, as (they claim) it represents choices women make and that it's unfair not to compare like with like. That misses the point on so many different levels as I will examine below. Very often what lies behind women's apparent choices is not freedom of choice but necessity, obstacles and prejudice.

The globalisation gap

I get that globalisation has raised many people out of poverty but many people are still drowning in it, particularly women and children.

Here's something to think about when you next look at the chocolate bars so deliciously arrayed in the supermarket.

Over 90% of Cocoa Farmers in the Cote' D'Ivoire are paid less than half what the World Bank deems a "living income" of a princely $2.50 a day. Yes, you read that right.

But the additional wrinkle here is that men take home $0.78c (US) per day, and women $0.25c. That is 10% of the "living income." Clearly, neither are anywhere near acceptable.

The sports gap

Forgive the abrupt jump here to what is a world of incomparable privilege. I'm including it here to show the distorting effects of averages and also because ignoring it is not going to help the starving cocoa farmers. I'm also including it because (as I subsequently point out) these distortions send powerful and toxic messages to girls and women.

No-one here is going to starve, but there are huge distortions in earnings in sport, in the prize money given to female athletes vs male athletes.

In the United Kingdom, in football, the 2021-22 FA Cup gives men a pot of £15.9 million and women £428,915.

The 2022 Football World Cup will see men given £335 million, compared to the £46 million women anticipate in 2023.

The 2021-22 Champions League gives men £1.66 billion and women £20 million.

In golf: men won £9.48 million in the US Open and women £7.59 million. The PGA Tour sees men receive £323.9 million and women £67.44 million.

The PGA Tour sees men receive £323.9 million and women £67.44 million. In tennis, in Dubai, men won £2.12 million and Women £530,744, in Melbourne men won £395,234 whereas women got £181,669.

The prize for the most enormous gap goes to the boxing world. In April 2022 Katie Taylor and Amanda Serrano fought at Madison Square Gardens - the biggest fight in women's boxing history. According to Jake Paul, Serrano's promoter, the fight had the second highest grossing boxing presale in the venue's 140-year history. It was also watched by millions of paying viewers around the globe. It was likened to the fight between Floyd Mayweather and Manny Pacquiao, a fight where Mayweather was estimated to have made over $300 million and Pacquiao over $100 million.

So what did the women make?

Estimates vary. The promoters themselves say "seven figures," i.e. somewhere between $1 million and $10 million dollars.[22] Much nearer the $1 million I suspect. Either way, a fraction of what Merryweather and Pacquiao made.

The cyclist Dame Laura Kenny, Team GB's most successful female Olympian, noted in the Daily Telegraph's campaign to close the pay gap in sport: "What message does this send society about women's sport and women? As female athletes we put in the same number of hours and make the same sacrifices, yet the rewards are completely different. Equal pay is a widely accepted principle in the workplace – it's time for sport to catch up."[23]

Sport is a great communicator that reaches across class, ethnicity, nations and genders. The message it is sending out to girls and boys, to women and men about the role of girls and women in society is profoundly unequal and deeply toxic and needs to change.

The disparity in earnings highlighted by the sports gap is an extreme example of the gaps that still persist in other spheres.

Why do these earnings gaps exist?

The answers seem to lurk in a smorgasbord of factors ranging from entrenching obstacles to women in the workplace in the form of prejudice and bias, conscious and unconscious on the part of both men and women, to structural and practical obstacles which encompass the ability to travel safely to and from work, the ability to work in a safe environment and the ability to balance work with caring responsibilities (notably childcare and caring for aged or sick family members), to historic legacies such as women not being able to compete in certain sports at high level until relatively recently.

Let's look at some of these factors.

The Motherhood pay gap

Equal Pay Day for mothers.

There is yet another dimension which in this case compares earnings for mothers versus fathers. US data[24] shows that on average, in 2018 mothers earned $0.69 for each $1 earned by fathers, so in 2019 their equal pay day was June 10.

Prof Claudia Goldin[25] analysing the earnings of men and women with

MBAs (Masters in Business Administration) found that "female MBAs earned considerably less than their male counterparts because the high paying corporate and financial sector positions heavily penalise employees who have even brief career disruptions and those who do not work exceptionally long and gruelling hours."

Goldin notes that at 3 to 4 years after the birth of the first child, a female MBA's earnings drop on average to 74% of the pre-birth levels. She contrasts this with women MBAs without children (married or not) who earn about 9 cents on the dollar less than their male counterparts (with or without children). Goldin calls these professions *greedy jobs.*

This care gap and its financial ramifications show up across the world, even in countries we might regard as in the forefront of gender equality, such as Denmark.

A Danish study pointed to an effective 20% motherhood earnings gap over the course of a mother's career compared to that of a father.[26]

Henrik Kleven of Princeton University discovered a sharp decline in women's earnings after the birth of their first child. Men however saw no comparable drop.

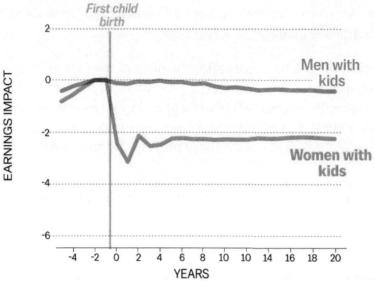

Women's earnings drop significantly after having a child. Men's don't.

Source: "Children and gender inequality: Evidence from Denmark," National Bureau of Economic Research

Vox

Kleven's research suggests that the gender pay gap might be more accurately termed a motherhood pay gap. His research and studies conducted in the US[27] show that women without children have earnings much closer to those of men.[28]

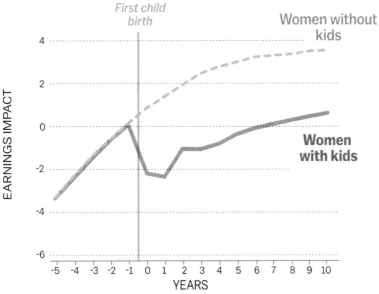

Having a kid correlates with lower earnings for women

Source: "Children and gender inequality: Evidence from Denmark," National Bureau of Economic Research

Childbearing, the study estimates, accounts for 80 percent of the gender wage gap in Denmark. The "motherhood penalty" in the US is estimated to cost women $16,000 a year in lost wages.[29] **Mothers in the US get paid 71 cents for every dollar their male counterparts make.** The survey also notes that employers view them as less devoted to their jobs than non-mothers.

Why do such preconceptions persist?

Presenteeism: outmoded patriarchal work practices

Personal note

When I worked as an investment banker, a trick perfected by my male colleagues, and for quite a few years all of my colleagues were male, was to leave their suit jacket on the back of their chair and scoot off surreptitiously. Their jackets hinted that they were hard at work, perhaps convened in a meeting room with all the other hard workers whose jackets decorated the back of their chairs. As opposed to at the pub.

The perception persists that *being there* equates to doing a good job and that being there *more* equates to doing an even better job.

A report in October 2021 by the charity Working Families noted that a third of mothers said that it was the people who worked the longest hours that were most respected by senior managers in their organisation. The study noted that almost 50% of parents with young children did not believe that senior leaders in their organisations were good role models for choosing a healthy work-life balance. We shall analyse later how companies with a more diverse group of employees who likely bring to the table more diverse work practices contribute to higher profitability than more homogeneous workplaces. That's just looking at the profit motive. If we wish to judge by other metrics such as a healthy work-life balance and the ability to bring up a family or care for older family members without putting extreme stresses on employees of whatever gender, then this mania with presenteeism needs to change.

The cost of having children and the consequences for parental participation in the workforce

According to a report by The Organisation for Economic Cooperation and Development (OECD), the UK is among the worst countries in the developed world for young mothers seeking work.

The report notes that the UK, along with the US, Ireland and New Zealand, scored lowest out of its 35 member states for this demographic, especially when women are in a couple without access to state subsidies. It said women were on average 1.4 times more likely to be not in education, employment or training (NEET) than men. The report noted that for many women this was because they were looking after young children and facing high childcare costs which proved a major barrier to employment. The report adds that "in the United States, Ireland, United Kingdom and New Zealand, childcare costs for a lone parent can account for between one-third and a half of net income."[30] Anecdotally, Alice

Thompson, writing in *The Times* (13/10/2021), cites visiting a cousin in Berlin who pays £42 a month for her two children's nursery school. That compares with £1500 a month for childcare in London. The cousin simply cannot afford to return to London. Again necessity determines causes of action. This is not free choice. It is not surprising that fertility rates in the United Kingdom are falling, down to 1.53 children per women from 2 children for women in 2000. Many women /couples decide they simply cannot afford to have children.

It would appear that women are the ones whose careers take a back seat more often than men to accommodate childcare responsibilities and also women who appear to be the ones more likely to pay for childcare rather than sharing the costs with our partners. A study conducted by The Fawcett Society and Scottish Widows in 2016[31] notes: "Many of the women described childcare as a cost paid from their incomes rather than as shared with their partners. This significantly limited their disposable income and ability to save for retirement."

Why is this? Could it be a lingering perception that if we choose not to fulfill our historic role as a full-time mother at home then we need to meet the cost of paying someone to surrogate for us? Of course it's possible that we women pay for childcare and our partners pay for other household bills.

The stark reality is that childcare is unaffordable for many women and gives us no real choice about working or not working if we have children.

The UK government has made some progress towards helping parents. Families getting certain government support can receive 15 hours free childcare for children age 2. And for eligible families with children aged 3 and 4 there is 15 hours free childcare available. Eligible working parents of children aged 3 to 4 years old receive 30 hours free childcare in England, though this stops when the child starts in reception class or reaches compulsory school age. Subsidies continue after age 11 (or 16 if disabled) whereby eligible parents can receive a subsidy of up to £2,000 per child per year. A helpful article by Johanna Noble, editor of The Times Money Mentor, updated as of July 2022, is referenced below.[32]

The government could give further support to working parents by making childcare and domestic help tax-deductible.

This would reduce the burden which falls unduly heavily on women. It would make it more affordable for women to go out to work and more permissible psychologically to employ someone to give that crucial help. Furthermore, it would put a monetary value on what has typically been unpaid: it might just make the contribution register in the eyes of those for whom it has been invisible. Plus, should any further justification be needed, women who employ domestic support will be creating work for someone who might not otherwise have had it. You could argue that this is trickle-down economics at work. And the person doing that cleaning or childcare is overwhelmingly likely to be female and in many cases a mother herself, fitting in such work around her own schedule.

Greedy jobs and their impact on the earnings gap

The fact is, many jobs have unpredictable hours, especially the higher paid jobs that Claudia Goldin called *greedy jobs*. In her excellent book *Career and Family*[33], Goldin cites those jobs, combined with the choices parents make to accommodate work and family, as one of the main reasons behind the persistence of earnings gaps. Typically the requirements of higher-earning jobs such as finance, law, or medicine, distort "couple equity". Goldin reports that while both parents in a partnership might set out with a goal to share childcare responsibilities equally, the nature of these jobs makes that choice economically inefficient.

These professions tend to reward those who can be *on call* professionally 24/7, effectively drop everything at a moment's notice to pull all-nighters, win a mandate, or push a project over the line. The extra hours here are not just rewarded pro-rata, they are rewarded disproportionately. Per hour, these on call, flexible individuals will earn more than those who work shorter hours, the ones who are *on call* for parenting. They will also win promotion; more so than those who work fewer hours.

The reality of parenting is that no matter how rich you might be, no matter how much childcare you can afford, one parent will need to be flexible and on call. The reality of greedy jobs means that it makes more economic sense not to share roles, but to specialise. One parent is on call for family, the other for work. The latter parent earns more and gets promoted more. The more family orientated parent earns less, gets promotes less, perpetuating and accelerating the earnings gap between them.

Typically the parent who make the choice to step back is the woman.

Personal note

When I was an investment banker I had no idea what my hours would be most days, just that they'd be a minimum of ten, often as much as fifteen. I could not have held down the jobs I did if I'd had children or I would not have been prepared to do so as the cost would have been too much on my children and on myself.

I was already a writer when I married and had my first of three children and most of the time could control my own hours, yet I could not envisage having written readable books without having help, given the demands of three children and family life, especially given that my husband travelled abroad for large chunks of time and that I had no family nearby. Having a nanny helped me work and helped my sanity though I feel guilty even writing this. Why is that?

"A woman must have a room of her own and money if she is to write fiction," said Virginia Woolf. Childcare also helps.

Workplace culture makes us step down

The cost of childcare and also the impossibility of childcare to realistically cover the insane working hours of certain occupations, means that these occupations are ruled out for many parents. I chose to rule myself out as an investment banker before having children and it's reasonable to suggest that the workplace culture of certain occupations will act as a deterrent to women, as the next section will show. That these are typically the higher paying occupations will clearly have an impact on the calculation of average earnings by gender.

Another contributing factor to pay gaps is *the workplace gap.*

The workplace gap

This measures wage equality, seniority and participation in the labour force.

A study by McKinsey[34] in the United States showed that in corporate America, women are underrepresented at every level, with women of colour being the most underrepresented, lagging behind white men, men of colour and white women. It's not, according to the study, lack of education or attrition rates which explain this. It starts at the beginning, where women are less likely to be recruited into entry-level jobs than men, despite enjoying a higher proportion of undergraduate degrees than men. The study revealed that only 85 women get promoted to manager for every 100 men who make it. This workplace gap was even bigger for some women, with 71 Latina women promoted compared to 100 men and 58 black women compared to 100 men. This makes me wonder: *Do we still live in the world depicted by the movie* Hidden Figures?[35]

And this is not because more women drop out. The attrition rate is the same.

The broken rung

McKinsey describes this as a *broken rung on the ladder.*

The lack of entry level women means that the pool from which the company can promote women is smaller than the pool of men. *Why are we being kept out of these jobs? Is it prejudice, conscious or unconscious? Could it also be that we are choosing to stay at away from these jobs? Is the workplace culture that has been created by generations of men just too inhospitable?*

External Bias

Sheryl Sandberg, former COO of Facebook, argues that when you account for differences in hours spent in the workforce, level of experience and the nature of the job there is still a whopping 38% of the pay gap that cannot be explained by the above factors. She concludes that *"It is bias… It is gender… There is no other explanation."*[36]

The Care Gap

Covid 19 has made things even more difficult for women. Research by McKinsey[37] has long shown that women carry much more of the housework and childcare burden than men. Data from the US shows that mothers were over three times as likely to be responsible for most of the housework and caregiving than men during the pandemic. The chart shows that for families with children under the age of 10, 22% of female corporate employees surveyed were putting in an additional five hours or more daily compared with 10% of male employees. The Care Gap strikes again.

Exhibit 4

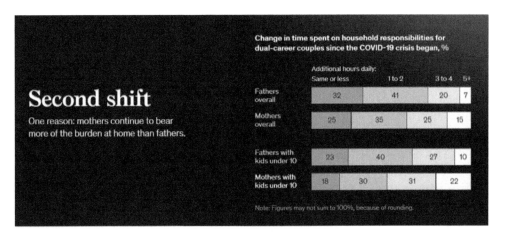

Source: Mckinsey

What has been evident for some decades is that women's entry into the paid workforce has not been met by a commensurate decrease in the hours of childcare and housework we put in. ***This creates a situation where for many of us we have no choice but to work part-time if we are going to accommodate these responsibilities.*** This is not an effective choice. This is for many, a necessity born of social conditioning and social restraints, some of them conscious, some of them unconscious.

According to the IMF, globally women do three times the amount of unpaid care work men do. This can be further subdivided into twice as much childcare and four times as much housework.

The costs of the care gap to our physical, mental and financial health

This care gap manifests in a workload in the office and at home, and the insane balancing act required, which in turn, manifests as stress. In 2017 the UK Health and Safety Executive reported that women had higher rates of work-related stress, anxiety and depression than men across all age ranges. On average, women were 53% more stressed than men, but in the age range of 35 to 44, which roughly coincides with when we have young children, the rate of stress suffered by women was nearly twice that suffered by men: 2,250 cases per 100,000 workers, compared to 1,270 per 100,000.

Financial consequences of the care gap

A recent OECD study[38] found that the gender pay gap in hourly wages is substantially higher in countries where women spend a large amount of time on unpaid care compared to men. No surprise there.

As we have seen, the Covid 19 pandemic has worsened the care gap with the result that one in three mothers, or an estimated two million women, have considered leaving the workforce. This will be mirrored around the world.

This contributes to women facing extreme poverty in our old age. Many of us just can't afford to save for it.

The caring roles that we choose for ourselves or which we have enforced upon ourselves clearly have a massive impact upon what we earn.

So does ruling ourselves out of certain jobs because we choose not to subject ourselves to the associated workplace cultures.

The persistence of patriarchally formed workplace cultures makes us swerve away from some of the higher paid arenas, such as investment banking and law, where more hours are worn as a badge of masochistic pride and rewarded disproportionately by senior management, elevating short-term target achievement above sustainable long term work practices. Many of us rule ourselves out before going there or we step aside when we start to have children. These environments do not lead to a healthy, happy, balanced life for people of whatever gender. They lead to more money but at what cost? The toxic, *suck it up,* investment banking culture is one that I knew well and from which I ran screaming (with joy to have escaped!). Perhaps it's time that we started challenging the assumptions that people need to pull an 80-hour week in order to do their job well. If we all attempt to do this, we can begin or accelerate the process of creating a healthier corporate culture which fosters a healthier personal work life balance.

We need to change this from within, both for our own sakes and for those who will come after us.

To sum up

Gender pay gaps are still going strong, often as a result of the choice that is often not a choice, as a result of the motherhood penalty or the care gap, where women take on a much heavier domestic burden than men which makes working full-time outside the home a compromise at best and impossible as worst. There is also a significant range of different pay gaps by ethnicity with, in general, women of colour more likely to suffer from bigger gaps. Gender pay gaps also persist because of biases and the *broken rung on the ladder* to higher-earning jobs within organisations, and because society has not caught up with female emancipation and participation as seen in women's sports such as football, golf, tennis and more.

What governments need to do:

- Make childcare more affordable. This means higher subsidies and more workplace creches
- Make the costs of cleaners and domestic helpers tax deductible
- Collect more data on the care gaps – who is spending how long caring for whom – and publicise it so that the costs and benefits of this care can inform decisions made by couples, corporates and society at large and can in turn help to influence government policy

What companies need to do:

- Promote more women and women of colour to achieve greater diversity which will help bring on other women and create changes in the workplace culture and establish role models and channels of opportunity for younger women
- Be more transparent: publicise more segregated earnings data by gender, ethnicity, class, sexuality, and disability to make it easier for us to call out the relevant gaps and correct them
- Recognise how 'greedy jobs' distort couple equity and look at structuring and enabling more flexible work practices

What we can do:

To make childcare more affordable

- Both parents can look at condensing their hours (5 days over 4 for example: if you both do it, then it saves you two days childcare)
- Take advantage of the tax free childcare scheme which will save you up to a possible 20% on your childcare
- And if you're only just over the threshold, put more in your

pension to bring it back under which is a double advantage

To improve the corporate environment

- Challenge the patriarchal workplace cultures of presenteeism and the inflexibility of greedy jobs
- Explore the possibility of unconscious factors holding us back, either on our own part or that of others

It is to our psychology and the belief systems that we grow up with around entitlement and ambition that we turn now.

Chapter Two: The Aspiration Gap

Conditioning, entitlement and ambition

How toxic taboos are still holding us back

The enduring legacy of patriarchal belief systems

What we can do about it

- The messaging sent to boys and girls reinforces and perpetuates harmful gender disparities. This manifests early and repeatedly, compounding into powerful and damaging conscious and unconscious beliefs

- People's financial habits are formed before the age of seven and above the age of three

- A 9% gender pocket money gap exists in the UK at age 11. In the US, that gap is 50%

- 64% of boys are taught by their parents about money, only 54% of girls are

- Parents feel much more comfortable talking about money to their sons than to their daughters

- Parents interrupt their daughters more than their sons

- Young boys interrupt girls twice as often as girls interrupt them

- Boys receive significantly more attention from teachers in class

- Care of Primark's range of gendered children's clothes,[39] girls are exhorted to be grateful, humble, good... told that kindness always wins. While boys are born to win, exhorted to change the game, rewrite the rules, to go for it. To explore...that there is nothing holding them back. That they are limitless.

- Male graduates of Russell group universities earn £28,000 fifteen months after leaving, while female graduates earn £24,000. By age 30 the gender graduate pay gap has increased to 25%40

- Male graduates earn on average £430,000 more than non-graduates over their lifetime

- Female graduates earn £260,000 more over their lifetime than non-graduates

- Women are less confident with job applications than men

- Women expect to be paid less

- Women are much less likely to request a pay rise than men

- Nearly 20% of men requested a rise twice or more each year. Only 8% of women did the same

- In meetings, men speak for longer, ask more questions and interrupt more than women do

I'm going to dive into psychology now, the psychology of our parents which is passed on to us which explains part of the gender pay gaps that we see in adulthood.

We looked in the previous chapter at what are called **negative freedoms**: our ability to act without hindrances such as prejudice, lack of safety, closed doors, glass ceilings, legal constraints or prohibitions.

But there's another force that's also holding us back from our full potential, both self-actualising and financial:

> *Positive freedoms* - **the freedoms we give ourselves, where we are liberated from internal constraints such as self-limiting beliefs.**

These are often a consequence of social conditioning which cuts across both negative and positive freedoms. The social conditioning received by others can constrain our ambitions because of discrimination and bias against us, whether conscious or unconscious.

What we shall see is that our positive freedoms are less than those enjoyed by men. And by boys.

Let's take a look at another pay /earnings gap, one which starts at a crucial time and will accordingly shape our beliefs around money and earnings.

The pocket money gender gap

Yes, this is a thing. Some might say it's small and trivial, but it is not. It helps shape perceptions about self and our relationship with money that will last for a lifetime. And limit us for a lifetime. It moulds expectations and beliefs, be they conscious or unconscious. And it is the unconscious beliefs that we carry forward that can do the most damage – for how do we fight an invisible enemy?

The gender pay gap starts disconcertingly early. A report compiled by *Go Henry* in 2019[41] analysed the financial habits of 75,000 British children aged 6 to 18. Those children collectively earned £4.5 billion from chores, pocket money and gifts. The report identified a pocket money gap of 5% with boys earning on average £440 a year versus £420 for girls. This gap peaks at 11 year old boys, earning £404 compared to girls earning £371: equivalent to 9% more.

A separate survey in the United States by *BusyKid*[42] reveals a much bigger gap. It shows that boys get twice as much pocket money as girls, receiving $13.80 compared to $6.71 for girls. Plus, boys get even bigger bonuses from their parents, receiving $17.01 compared to $15.54 for girls. It would seem that boys have more opportunities for making money from jobs. [An interesting side report suggests that boys were more likely to spend their cash while girls were more likely to give it to charity.]

BusyKid CEO Greg Murset regarded this as "an important wake-up call", commenting: "I don't think any parent would intentionally pay differently based on gender, but clearly, it's happening."

But why? Could it be that the expectation is that girls help out around the house so don't *warrant* payment for it whereas boys need to be *incentivised* to do so? Or are more tasks seen as appropriate to boys than girls and pushed their way? Some of the parents and children to whom Go Henry spoke suggested it is because boys are more pushy than girls about asking for money. This starts and foreshadows a pattern that shows up in the workplace (I come to this later) which shows that women are less likely than men to ask for pay rises.

Either way these are not healthy dynamics to be instilling consciously or subconsciously into our children. These early gaps and biases are formative. A study from the University of Cambridge[43] found that people's financial habits are formed before the age of seven and above the age of three. The Cambridge research found that financial confidence gained then will carry through to adulthood. As will the lack of financial confidence, as we shall see below.

If we wonder from where other aspects of confidence might derive, look no further than Primark's range of gendered children's clothes.[44] Girls are exhorted to be "grateful, humble and optimistic," to "be good, do good." They are told that "kindness always wins." And boys… they are told they are "born to win", exhorted to "change the game. Rewrite the rules. Go for it." To "explore." And for good measure, they are told that there is "Nothing holding you back. You are Limitless."

Harmless? Trivial? I don't think so.

The graduate pay gap and the ethnicity employment gap

These gender gaps in pay /income continue apace when students leave university. Just 15 months after graduation, men earned on average 10% more than women.[45] And even where graduates had similar qualifications a wide pay gap opened up.

And the more elite the university, the bigger the gap. Data covering Russell Group universities including Oxford and Cambridge show that on average male graduates earn £28,000 fifteen months after leaving, compared to women's £24,000. The authors of the report state that this gap "is not accounted for by subject of study, type of university attended, prior attainment, social background or ethnicity."

Results from the survey also showed an ethnicity employment gap, with only half of black university graduates in full-time employment more than a year after they left, compared with more than 60% of white students.

Another study in 2021 by The Institute for Fiscal Studies reports that by age 30 the gender graduate pay gap in annual earnings has increased to 25%.[46] The same study reports that male graduates earn on average £430,000 more than non-graduates over their lifetime, while female graduates earn £260,000 more over their lifetime than non-graduates.

So what accounts for this graduate gender pay gap?

The answer is nuanced. The authors of the Higher Education Policy Institute Report state that "women are more likely to look for job security, work-life balance, a good company culture and a job that enables them to contribute to a cause they believe is meaningful." They imply that for a larger proportion of men, a high salary is the main criterion. They also note that "men appear to be more focused on their career search than women – they begin their career planning earlier during their time at university, make more applications and are less likely to give up once they've begun an application. They also display more confidence and are more speculative in the jobs they apply for."

Yet, despite and perhaps even because of this, the authors note *"women are more likely to be offered a job once interviewed and are less likely to be unemployed on graduating."* They suggest that this may be because women are more efficient but they also suggest it might be because we are less ambitious. They note that *"women expect less pay than men."* That poses the question:

Why do we expect less pay?

Are we too busy being "good... grateful, humble and always perfect?" while the guys are "changing the game, exploring, rewriting the rules. Going for it... with nothing holding them back, because they are limitless...?"[47]

And it raises another question:

Are employers getting us on the cheap?

Another explanation could be that women are more likely to work in part-time employment both during and immediately after their degree.

Whatever the reason for this, it perpetuates the tendency we see throughout a woman's working life – she is much more likely to work part-time than a man. And inevitably it begs another question: *is this choice or is this necessity?*

Limits remain on our positive freedoms - the Aspiration Gap made visible

Time to explore positive freedom - our freedom to act without being constrained by self-limiting beliefs whether they be conscious or unconscious.

Co-author of the Higher Education Policy Institute Report, Bethan Cornell, makes a fascinating observation. She says "At the time of writing this report I was… searching for jobs… And the conclusions we made completely changed my attitude to job-hunting. Learning about the graduate gender pay gap and the possible reasons behind it has been utterly empowering and has altered my approach. Seeing the difference in confidence levels and values between the average male and female graduates has assured me that I have the right to be ambitious in terms of pay and that I should be more assertive in applying for higher paid roles. While writing the report, I made a successful application to a well-paid role that I definitely would not have even considered applying to before starting this research."

In its attempt to explain the graduate pay gap, The Institute for Fiscal Studies cites both negative and positive freedoms. The study notes that by age 30, subject choice explains only a fifth of the total gender pay gap. They posit that other contributing factors could include "motherhood, gender differences in attitudes towards risk, recognition for group work, hours worked, the propensity to bargain over wages and ask for promotions, and discrimination."[48] Again, the confidence gap holds us back from negotiating on our own behalf.

Again, our own levels of self-belief are potentially getting in our way. It's not surprising that we should limit our beliefs in this way when we are being told consciously and unconsciously by external forces that certain subjects are more appropriate for us than others, that certain jobs are more appropriate for us than others, that certain behaviours are more appropriate for us than others, that, for example, we should not push ourselves forward or be "aggressive," that this is not "womanly" behaviour. This is particularly pernicious when it comes to money.

Women and the money taboo

Some taboos are there for a good reason, they form the basis of much of our morality. Others, like Sade's mellifluous song, might be sweet. This one is toxic.

Toxic taboo

There is a generalised money taboo but it manifests more strongly and perniciously with women than with men. A 2018 YouGov report commissioned by Lloyds Bank[49] showed that 50% of UK adults believe that talking about money matters is taboo in everyday conversation, higher than the sex (42%), religion (26%), or politics (14%).

Money is even more off-limits for girls. A study by HSBC[50] showed that while 64% of boys are taught by their parents about money only 54% of girls are. **The parents surveyed said they felt much more comfortable talking about money to their sons than to their daughters.**

If money is deemed "unfeminine" then clearly it is going to be much harder for us to ask for pay rises. We are hardwired by our history not to ask for our due.

Personal note

One of the things I feel most uncomfortable about with my own work is setting out the cost of what I charge for speaking appearances and workshops. I'm an ex-investment banker used to negotiating deals. I was taught by experts, mentored by ninjas. I was a good negotiator, on the bank's behalf. However, when it comes to negotiating my own lecture fees, I find it agonising. Neither my training nor my awareness has not enabled me to shake off the legacy of the money taboo. I still have to fight against it and when I do, I still feel deeply uncomfortable and I have no doubt that were I a man, I would negotiate for, and almost certainly be paid, *more*.

And I know I'm not the only one. I was talking to a female literary agent and she told me she was an absolute ninja when it came to negotiating deals on behalf of her clients but that when it came to her own remuneration, she had never once in 20 years asked for a pay rise…

Impostor Syndrome

I suspect another force is at work here, one with which many women will identify: impostor syndrome.

If the very act of negotiating for promotion or a bigger salary is deemed unfeminine, aggressive, shameful or beyond our worth, then it's not surprising we shy away from doing so.

And we do. Big time. A study carried out by Good Money Week[51] found nearly a third of women feel "awkward" about asking for more money but just a fifth of men feel uncomfortable.

41 per cent of men had talked about a salary rise with their manager in the last six months, whereas just a third of women had.

More than a quarter of women interviewed had *never* requested a pay rise.

Nearly 20% of men requested a rise twice or more each year. Only 8% of women did the same.

Sam Smethers, Chief Executive of women's rights organisation Fawcett Society, said: "Women spend their lives conditioned not to be 'pushy' and to put others before themselves, so it's not surprising that this plays out in the workplace."

Charlene Cranny, campaigns director at Good Money Week, said: "It's probably not a huge shock to anyone reading this that women are still more likely than men to feel awkward broaching the subject of money. Our research suggests that men have no qualms in instigating these conversations with employers more regularly and in turn, they are receiving higher and more regular pay rises, and we feel that it is time to redress the balance."

Amen to that. The more we can get out of our comfort zones and do this the easier it will get both for us and for female colleagues and for the women who come after us.

These aren't the only conversations where male voices are in the ascendant.

We are heard less than men

In meetings, men speak for longer, ask more questions and interrupt more than women. Mary Ann Sieghart in her excellent *Authority Gap* cites multiple studies.

Researchers from Brigham Young University and Princeton[52] reported that at a mixed table, men will dominate the conversation, taking up 75 per cent of the conversation, and leaving just 25 per cent of the talking to women. They found that "increasing numbers of women can help women's voices be heard, but you really need to get to a majority of women before you see a difference."

A separate study[53] of 250 academic seminars across 10 countries reported that men were 2.5 times more likely to ask a question than women. Researchers found that women were more likely to say they didn't have the confidence to ask or felt intimidated by the speaker, **but** if a woman asked the first question it would encourage more women to speak up.

Men also interrupt us on a frequent basis. A study of US Supreme Court Justices[54] found that although women made up one third of the justices they were subjected to two-thirds of all interruptions. Effectively, this meant that women were four times more likely to be interrupted than their male colleagues. It's also worth noting that this wasn't a case of women interrupting women. 96% of these interruptions were by men.

Sieghart points to further studies showing how teachers spend a disproportionate amount of time with boys, *eight times as much* - and that "girls are being ignored and shortchanged,"[55] that parents interrupt their daughters more than their sons[56] and that very young boys between the ages of 3½ and 5 interrupt girls twice as often as girls interrupt them.[57]

Sieghart also points out what I and many other female authors have known for a long time, to our cost, that men are MUCH less likely to read books by women than are women to read books by men.[58] This applies particularly to fiction but also to non-fiction.

I think it's fair to say that our voices are heard less than those of men. That's the best I can say. I could argue that we are being silenced from when we first begin to find our voices as toddlers, gagged by the precepts of the *good girl* who doesn't interrupt and speak up, and drowned out by the *normal boy* who feels able to do both.

It's heartening to see how men's behaviour changes if women are in a majority, where we are able to make ourselves heard. This has implications for both governmental and corporate policy. If you want to give women a voice that will be heard you need to massively increase their representation to at least half.

To sum up:

Gender pay gaps begin almost as soon as children are old enough to receive pocket money. Gender conditioning gaps also start from a young age, with girls being subjected to much more interruption from boys and from parents than boys are, with teachers giving boys much more classroom attention, and in the explicit messages that the different genders are sent. This is starkly visible on gendered clothes. Small, insignificant and trivial? I don't think so. This conditioning snowballs over time into something much bigger and deeply damaging. We see this evidenced in the graduate pay gap. Part of this seems to stem from graduates' own expectations and limiting self beliefs. This is particularly galling because you might think that these young people are carrying with them into the workforce a mentality of equality, an unwillingness to accept these kinds of aspiration and pay gaps.

The Fawcett Society believes it could take another 60 years to close the gender pay gap. Let's accelerate that pace. Knowledge empowers us to tackle these issues. Let's spread the word.

What we can do:

- Bring up our children as fairly as possible, aware of the biases and subconscious conditioning that we developed/were inculcated with as children so that we do not perpetuate those biases
- As teachers, be aware that our own subconscious biases might be distorting the airtime we give boys vs girls in our classrooms
- Break the money taboo, and talk to our children, particularly our girls, about money and financial literacy
- Inspire our girls to pursue careers that resonate with them, and arm them with the resources they need to pursue these jobs, one of which is self-belief, or at the very least, a 'fake it till you make it' mentality (which is not ideal but it's better than holding ourselves back)
- Boycott companies and retailers with toxic messages on their products
- If we are a manufacturer or a retailer, be aware of this toxic messaging and eliminate it
- Expand our own personal freedom by challenging our self-imposed limitations
- Get out of our comfort zones
- Apply for more ambitious jobs
- Ask our bosses for pay rises and promotions[59]
- Make our voices heard
- Increase the number of women in decision-making roles

Chapter Three: The Gender Pensions Chasm

We have much smaller pension pots than men.

Why that is

What we can do about it

- Women would have to work a staggering 37 years longer at the present rate of contributions in order to close the pension gap with men

- Because of differences in life expectancy, women actually need to save between 5 to 7% more than men

- In the UK, women in their 60s have an average of £51,100 in their private pension pots while men have £156,500

- Over two-thirds of pensioners living in poverty are women

- 1.2 million women approaching retirement age have no savings at all

- Divorced women's retirement savings averaged £26,100 compared with £103,500 for divorced men

- Single mothers have on average only £18,300 in their pension pots

- The pension mountain required to fund anything more than a hand to mouth existence in old age – now stands at more than £250,000

- The care gap and the propensity of women to work part-time plus the way the auto enrolment legislation has been crafted, explains around 50% of the pensions gap

- The gender pay gap itself accounts for a further 28 per cent[60]

- The remaining 22% would appear to be the result of a knowledge gap

- As many as 76% of women do not know how much they need to save for a comfortable retirement

- A study by Scottish Widows[61] estimated that women would have to work a staggering 37 years longer at the present rate of contributions in order to close the pension gap with men[62]

- A report by Legal and General[63], analysing the pension pot sizes of its four million pension scheme holders revealed a 17% pensions gap between men and women in their 20s, which widened to 34% by their 40s, to 51% by their 50s and to 56% by retirement

There is a pension crisis brewing globally.

Tens of millions of pensioners around the world are facing a retirement crisis due to underfunding, plunging interest rates and increases in average life expectancy. Covid has worsened an already bad situation. Women have been hit particularly hard because our pension pots are smaller, we live longer, and we have been hit disproportionately hard by the pandemic.[64] As of end May 2020, a report by The Institute for Fiscal Studies[65] showed that mothers were fifty percent more likely than fathers to have either lost or quit their job since the lockdown began in March 2019. Citibank estimates[66] that of the 44 million redundancies predicted worldwide, 31 million of them will be women, more than double the 13 million men.

This will make an already bad situation worse.

In the UK, women in their 60s have an average of £51,100 in their private pension pots while men have £156,500.

The situation is particularly dire for single mothers who have on average only £18,300 in their pension pots.[67] A subsequent report published on 21 March 2022 by Now: Pensions[68] claimed that as a result of the Covid pandemic single mothers' pension pots had fallen by 40% from £18,300 to just £11,000 and 58% of single mothers are now ineligible for a workplace pension.

It's not all bad news. Scottish Widows 2020 Adequate Savings Index showed that the gap between men and women has disappeared. 61% of women now save at least 12% of their income for retirement or are in a defined benefit pension scheme, the same as men. This is heartening. Pre 2011, only 40-45% of women were saving an adequate share of their income. Scottish Widows notes "much of this progress has likely been driven by policy reform including automatic enrolment, initiated in 2012."

While this is very welcome, gaps in pension savings from previous years still mean there will need to be a lot of catching up done before women close the overall pensions gap.

A report by trade union Unison, reveals

- Female pensioners have a net weekly income that is approximately 85% of their male counterparts
- Women account for approximately 61% of pensioners above state pension age
- Over two-thirds of pensioners living in poverty are women

The bitter irony is that while we save *less* for our pensions and than men we actually need to save *more*.

Life expectancy

Just 120 years ago, pensions were for many people an irrelevance. In the UK in 1900, men died at an average age 44 and women at 48.[69]

In happy contrast, as of 2017, the life expectancy for women was on average 82.9 years compared to 79.2 years for men (and babies born now are predicted to live on average more than a hundred years).

That means that even if our pension pots were the same, women would receive a lower annual pension than men due to the actuarial methods of calculation. Actuaries predict[70] that women need to save around 5 to 7% more than men in order to enjoy the same level of income in retirement.

The picture becomes gloomier still because given the demands of an ageing population the security of the UK state pension is open to doubt.

Whatever manifesto promises politicians might make, cold hard economic realities mean that we cannot rely on the state pension to bail us out or on once generous company pensions.

To a certain extent, the state's ability to honour pension commitments has been predicated on a kind of pension Ponzi scheme where the United Kingdom and many other countries are relying on birth rates higher than the replacement figure of on average, 2.08 children, to ensure long-term "natural" replacement of the population. Specifically the working population.

If you have a situation where you have a falling birth rate, as we do now, with the 2021 birth rate falling to an all-time low of 1.58, the lowest since records began in 1938, this implies a shrinking working population in decades to come, relative to the retired population (unless you fill those gaps with immigration).

As of 2021[71], there are a little under three over 65s for every ten workers, but by the middle of the next decade that ratio will rise to 3.5. By the 2060s the number will be closing to 4.

Meanwhile, by 2050 a quarter of Britons will be over 65, up from a fifth today. That should sound a siren warning about the state's ability to continue to fund pensions and increases in pensions along current lines and we've already seen the triple lock to pensions thrown into question.

We also see the implications of the falling birth rate in the microdynamics within families.

Historically and in many less-developed countries, women have relied, as have men, on children to act as their pensions by taking care of them in their old age but the statistics here, especially in the first world, are problematic. Women born in 1965 are twice as likely to be childless as the generation of women born at the end of the Second World War. Currently almost one third of over 85s receive regular care from their children[72] but the Office for National Statistics predicts that in 30 years' time tens of thousands of baby boomers will require care but will have no one to help them. Instead, they will have to depend on paid carers.[73]

This is a problem that the state needs to address. But need doesn't equate to action and the more we can do ourselves to provide for our old age, the better.

Before everything gets too pessimistic, one golden nugget is auto enrolment although as we shall see below this has a profound structural flaw which particularly disadvantages women.

Auto enrolment

Before auto enrolment came in, it was up to the individual to join their employer's pension scheme. Now under auto enrolment you are automatically put into your employer's workplace pension scheme although you can still choose to opt out. This is nudge economics.

Employers contribute a minimum of 3% of your salary (up to a cap of £50,000). You then are required or requested to contribute an extra 3% of your salary to your own pension up to a total of 8% of your pre-tax salary. The government contribution works by giving you tax relief. So if you wanted to get £100 put into a pension, if you are a basic rate taxpayer you would need to only pay in £80 because the tax authorities would effectively[74] add £20 to your pension pot. Higher rate taxpayers would only need to put £60 in to get a £100 contribution and top rate taxpayers only need to put in £55 for the government to top that up to £100.

By February 2019 more than 10 million workers had been auto enrolled. Fewer than 10% of those who were eligible had opted out. But that still left 9 million employees not in any workplace pension. The situation has improved more recently: by January 2020 the total number had reached 15 million and by August 2022 had increased by a further 9.6%, but with a wobble. The figure for opt outs was 10.4% in August 2022. The cited report[75] blames Covid for a rise from 7.6% in January 2020.

Auto-enrollment and women

However, one particular auto-enrollment rule particularly penalises women. Currently (as of August 2021) companies are required to enroll their employees in their own pension schemes only if they earn over £10,000 in one single job. This means that many part-time workers who earn less than £10,000 in any single job are excluded. Self-employed workers, those on flexing contracts, and those in the gig economy also fall outside this threshold.

Women are much more likely than men to work in part-time flexible jobs because of the demands of caring for young children or other dependent relatives. Data from the Office for National Statistics in 2019 showed that 39% of employed women worked part-time compared to 11% of employed men. The result is that of the 13.4 million employed women in the United Kingdom, 24% are not eligible for a staff pension compared to 15% of men.[76]

The self employed and pensions

If you are self-employed then auto enrollment will not be an option but there are various other channels through which you can set up your own pension. You could take out a Personal Pension, a Stakeholder Pension or you could set up a Self-Invested Personal Pension (SIPPs).

You can find out more on the following government website but there are also other sources of information available in useful resources at the end of the book.

https://www.yourpension.gov.uk/self-employment/

I will also be covering other forms of investing for retirement in later chapters.

Single women and pensions

31% of single mothers are not eligible for staff pensions which equates to 341,000 not paying into their pension and also missing out on employer contributions. The picture gets even worse as single mothers are also much less likely to own their own property, only 26% do compared with a national average of 65%. The harsh reality is that many single mothers are forced to sacrifice their career progression and earning ability to work around school drop-offs and pick-ups and holidays.

The reality of life as a single mother is laid bare in the £6,922 a year she earns working part time on average compared with £9,976 for women in general. The gender pensions gap is particularly cruel for the most vulnerable.

A report by the Resolution Foundation notes that this situation is worsened because a whopping 800,000 people who should be covered by the auto enrolment scheme are not either because their employers don't know or understand the rules or because they choose to ignore them. The same report adds that women were more likely than men to be under enrolled. This is particularly pernicious because of the compounding effect of missing out on years of pension contributions (see sections on investing).

Covid has made that even worse.

Covid 19 will have an adverse effect on everyone's pension pots but more so on women's than men. A higher proportion of job losses have been suffered by women than by men, and more women than men have reduced their working hours. The double whammy of this is that more women will fall below the £10,000 automatic employer pension contribution threshold in one job and those who have lost their jobs or have been forced to quit to take care of dependents will not be contributing to their pensions and will lose out on their employer contributions as well.

Even those who remain in work might well be hit. The Financial Times estimates in 2020 that up to £1bn in pension contributions could be suspended as businesses strike deals with retirement scheme trustees to keep afloat during the pandemic.

Virgin Atlantic, the airline owned by Richard Branson, and the Financial Times itself are among the employers who announced temporary cuts to staff pension payments, in response to Covid-19 pressures.

Auto-enrollment, though flawed, is a positive move but it is not sufficient by itself.

Mark Pemberthy, head of Defined Contribution Wealth Consultancy, Buck, notes that though it is "encouraging to see more people than ever participate in their workplace pension schemes, figures also show that most people are continuing to chronically underfunded their retirement." He stresses that most defined contribution schemes "are not designed to generate adequate retirement incomes and as a result most employees are not saving enough to buy the standard of living they want or expect in retirement." Research from the Pensions and Lifetime Saving Association showed in 2020 that 18 million people (56%) saving into a pension are not confident that they are saving enough to live the lifestyle they want when they retire.

So, neither men nor women are saving enough but the problem is particularly acute for women.

So why are we women not saving enough for our pensions?

The answers are interesting and nuanced. It's partially because we cannot and partially because we don't want to.

A survey by Scottish Widows and the Fawcett Society reveals that although having a family made women consider saving for a pension, the higher costs of family life got in the way. Having children hit many of the women interviewed in three ways.

1) They took time out of work for maternity leave
2) Some of them reduced their hours (and resultantly earnings) when they returned to work. Very few women had continued paying contributions into their occupational pension plans during this time out
3) The report notes that "participants were also unlikely to have considered how working part-time might affect their job progression, salary and therefore total pension pot."
4) The ongoing costs of childcare. Mystifyingly, many of the women paid for childcare from their incomes rather than sharing the cost with their partners.[77] This significantly impacted their ability to save for retirement. The report also notes: "Almost all the women in the study expressed a commitment to financial independence. However, when probed it emerged that women who had cut their contributions to meet the cost of care were often relaxed about this as they believed they could draw on their partner's pension."

But that's a risky decision. The bleak reality is that 41% of marriages end, with women hit much harder by divorce than men - experiencing a one third drop in income compared to one fifth for men[78]. The survey above shows the consequences of this: divorced women's retirement savings averaged £26,100 compared with £103,500 for divorced men.

The propensity of women to work part-time due to their responsibilities as carers for their children or elderly relatives plus the way the auto enrolment legislation has been crafted, explains around 50% of the pensions gap. The gender pay gap itself accounts for a further 28 per cent.[79]

So what explains the remaining 22%?

Here we enter the realm of awareness/ knowledge and psychology.

Even when women earn the same as men we still save less into our pensions and are more likely than men to say we don't understand pensions products.[80] As many as 76% of women do not know how much they need to save for a comfortable retirement.[81] A survey commissioned by Standard Life in 2022[82] shows that women are far more likely than men to have never reviewed their pension at 25% vs 13%. The study also shows that those on the lowest incomes are also the least likely to review their pensions. More than third – 34% – of those with an income of £10,000–£20,000 have never reviewed their pension, falling to 21% of those who earn £20,000–£30,000. This drops to 15% among those earning £30,000–£40,000 and 14% among people with an income of £40,000–£50,000.

So what's emerging here is that there is an **awareness/ knowledge gap** as well. We need to arm ourselves with information on **how** to invest in our pensions and **how much** we need to invest, and it's not the same as men either because we live longer. We'll come to the 'how to's' below and in subsequent chapters.

Pension psychology

One potential reason why women are saving less into our pension pots is that we **put ourselves and our own financial needs last.** One respondent to the Scottish Widows and the Fawcett Society report noted her own personal consequence of having a family.

"Your requirements sort of end up bottom of the pile."

To this I would say – put your own financial oxygen mask on first. If you are financially insecure it will affect not only your future but your day-to-day well-being and by implication that of your family.

Another reason is that we dislike saving via pensions, and in some ways, we don't regard it as actual saving.

"It's almost like another bill," said one respondent to the Scottish Widows and Fawcett Society survey. Pension contributions tend to be seen as a cost without a reward. Many participants view them as akin to paying a tax.

The study revealed that the women studied felt more motivated and satisfied adding to other forms of saving than to their pension pot.

The pension image problem

There is a tendency to view pensions as something we don't need to worry about for a long time, something that will look after itself, something we just don't need to bother with now. Many of us have a tendency to prioritise our current self over our future self.

Also, pensions have an image problem which I suspect will afflict both men and women.

When we are young and callow, the words *pension* and *pensioners* conjure up bent figures in tattered clothing hobbling along with sticks, eyes on the pavement. *Old Age Pension* is something you receive during those doddery days prior to death, a kind of living death when you are a zombie version of what you were before. No wonder we resent paying towards it, or find better uses for our money.

Apologies to all pensioners. The reality is not at all like that for most people. But words are powerful and images linger with all their negative associations and influence our behaviour to our detriment, even when we, in theory, know better.

Personal note

Early on in my marriage when my husband gamely tried to discuss our pension provisions, I banned the subject. I'd like to think I can talk across a wide range of conversational gambits but pensions were verboten. Immature, reckless, irresponsible, I was all of the above. Of course I *should* have been interested in pensions but whenever anyone uses the *should* word on me that also makes me want to run for the hills.

But an impoverished old-age is not very appealing either, is it? The young glamorous Carrie Bradshaw observed in *Sex and the City*: "I spent more than $40,000 on shoes but I have nowhere to live. I will be the ultimate old woman who lives in a shoe."

As Carrie intimates, there is nothing glamorous about a poverty–stricken old-age. We all really need to talk about the subject, and to provide for ourselves, much, much more generously.

The pension mountain

The pension mountain – the stack of cash required to fund anything more than a hand to mouth existence in old age – now stands at more than a quarter of a million pounds.

That's what we'll need to save on top of the full state pension, insurer Royal London has warned in a new research paper designed to shock government and consumers into increasing our woefully inadequate old age savings.

The figure is based on matching the average working income and takes into account spending changes like reduced travel costs because we'll no longer be commuting to work.

It's up by more than £100,000 since 2002 thanks to plummeting interest rates and rising life expectancy.

Smugness killed the pension

And despite auto-enrollment, the biggest overhaul to retirement saving in memory, we're nowhere close.

And now there's another issue threatening to scupper our best savings intentions – complacency.

The workplace pension scheme has undoubtedly swept significant numbers of people into saving for retirement. Around half of UK adults are now thought to be saving enough to favourably compare their pre- and post-retirement life. But for many others, the assumption that saving the minimum automatic contribution will be enough, coupled with precious little information on precisely how much their total pot needs to be worth, has stalled savings rates.

"This research has big implications for the mandatory 8 per cent contribution rate from April 2019 for those who have been enrolled into a workplace pension,"[83] says Helen Morrissey, personal finance specialist for Royal London.

"This is a great start, but the government needs to act quickly to nudge people up to more realistic savings levels. Without this, many millions of people will face a sharp drop in living standards when they retire."

Changing fortunes

Critically, those millions will include a disproportionate number of millennials whose other financial circumstances are already a step behind their older peers.

How to sort our pensions. What to do and how to invest

Start today.

It's easy to think *I'll get my finances sorted next year, I'll sort my debt next year, I'll sort my investments next year, I'll sort my pension next year* but time ticks away and it's not going to get any easier to step into your financial power. Sooner really is better thanks to the joys of compound returns and also the sense of empowerment harnessing your money and your spending can give you.

Think of it as getting free money today.

Rarely do we get free money. But here we do, both from our employers and from the government. Employers who match your contributions to your pension basically give you a 100% return on every pound you save into your pension plan. In addition, whatever tax threshold you meet, the government will adjust upwards your effective contribution. You're not going to get a return like that anywhere else, so take it up, as much as possible.

And what is the target to aim for?

- Start investing in a pension as soon as you possibly can
- Pay in a percentage of your income so that as your earnings increase, so do your pension contributions

The maths

In an ideal world, and as a rough guide, you need to pay in contributions equivalent to half your age, so if you're 25 the contributions should be 12.5% of your income going into your pension pot but if you're but if you're 38 when you start you need to pay 17% of your income in.

We often look at our budgets in terms of how much can we afford to spend, but we also need to ask ourselves how much can we afford to invest? We don't want to beggar ourselves or live a miserable lifestyle but we want to balance the future against the present, jam tomorrow versus jam today, deferred gratification against current pleasures.

But what if you live longer than average?

Let's do some comparisons. Let's assume you are 22 and you pay in a personal monthly pension contribution of £250 which is matched by an equal contribution from your employer (based on certain assumptions, see note.) If you include the state pension you would be projected to have an annual pension income on retirement of £30,682.

However if you start your pension five years later aged 27, your projected annual pension drops to £27,070. If you don't start paying in until you are 32 your annual projected pension drops to £23,825.

If you don't start paying in until you're 42 your annual expected pension drops to £18,278.

If we take the state pension out of this equation then for the last example your annual pension would be projected to be £9,168. If you started paying in at 32 that would go up to £14,715 and at 27 years old it would be £17,960 and 22 years old it would be £21,571.

Pension Bee has a helpful approach. Its pension calculator asks you your age when you start saving, how much you and your employer pay in and how much you want per year when you retire. It also tells you how long this pension pot will last. For example, if you're 27, you plan to retire at 65, your desired retirement income is £32,000 a year, your monthly contribution is £430 and your employer's monthly contribution is £250 then its calculations report that you'd be on track to have £471,683 at retirement. This would potentially provide you with £32,000 per year, but at this rate it would only last until you were eighty eight years old. So if you have good longevity genes you might want to invest more or take out less every year.

But what if we don't want to wait that long for a pension. What if we want to retire at 50? How much do we need to invest monthly to get that £30,000? The answer is £650 a month with a £250 employer contribution. This includes the state pension.

With more modest monthly savings, the figures look bleak.

Of course we can supplement our savings for our old age in other ways and I will explore those later in the book.

Caveat emptor – buyer beware

Pensions and fraud

We need to look at another aspect of pensions which is using and protecting the pension pot that we do have. One think tank[84] suggests that more than £2 trillion worth of our pension pot cash is vulnerable to fraudsters. The police foundation found that analysing just 13 pension providers, £54 million worth of pension wealth was thought to have been targeted by scammers in 2019 with £31 million of that likely to have been lost.

The issue here is when we transfer our pension from existing providers to other providers that we think could manage it better, 62% of people, even when warned about the risks of transferring the pension, have done so. Clearly it makes sense to transfer our pension pots away from poorly performing managers but we have to be incredibly careful we are actually transferring them to a genuine fund manager not to a fraudster. Regulators need to do more to tackle fraud and to potentially block the transfer if they believe it is fraudulent but given that the Police Foundation[85] estimates that £2.5 trillion of the total £6.1 trillion of pension wealth in the UK was "accessible" to fraudsters, we need to be careful. Typically, these frauds begin with a phone call offering you what would appear to be a good deal on switching your pension. The best thing you can do is hang up. Never take unsolicited calls of this nature. If you are thinking of transferring your pension, then see below.

To sum up:

A pension crisis is brewing globally although it is affecting women more than men, leaving us far more exposed to an impoverished old age. We are in a particularly perilous position because of a combination of the pay gap which gives us less money to begin with, an understanding gap where we are not as financially literate as men, and also because of structural defects in the auto-enrollment programme whereby it does not kick in until we earn more than £10,000 in a single job. Motherhood also exacerbates the pension gap as does any interruption to our workplace life as it's likely that we will stop paying pension contributions during that interruption. It is also likely that such interruptions will have long-term implications for our earning capacity and promotions within the workplace. Typically it is women who take such interruptions as a result of having children. Typically we rely on our partner's contributions to make up for our temporary opting out. I'm not going to knock operating on trust but I would just say that it harks back to the situation prevalent with inheritance laws before reform when we relied on the good nature and sense of fairness of men for our financial well-being rather than having it enshrined ourselves either by our own actions or by our own legal position. I would also add that many such 'temporary' optings out become permanent especially if women have more than one child, when the costs and stresses of the juggling act simply can become unsustainable. But many of those women who do continue working after having had children also erode the amount they can invest in their pensions because they pay exclusively for child care themselves rather than splitting the costs with their partner. This makes me wonder why this should be the case. Could it be from some residual sense of guilt whereby we feel that we really ought to be staying home to take care of our children and if we are not then the very least we can do is pay 100% of the cost of someone else doing it? Anecdotally, it appears that it is women not men who overwhelmingly pay their cleaners from their own earnings, perhaps from the same residual sense that if they are going to subcontract the work their gender always used to do and perhaps is still expected to do, then they need to pay for it, both figuratively and literally.

Covid has made the situation worse. Women were more likely to lose their jobs, see a reduction in hours or find themselves forced to quit the workplace altogether because of the unsustainable stresses of trying to combine family and work life under lockdown.

What government needs to do:

- Make provision for women (and men) who do not earn above the £10,000 threshold in any one job to be auto enrolled
- Act quickly to nudge people up to more realistic savings levels to protect them from a sharp drop in living standards on retirement

What companies need to do:

- The financial services industry must provide women with tailored advice when advising either single women or married couples on retirement given our longer average life expectancies
- It needs to reflect gender diversity among its clients by recruiting and training more female advisers

What we can do:

- Start saving early and start as big as possible
- Recognise the importance of our own financial health and act on it. If we are financially insecure it will affect not only our future but our day-to-day well-being and by implication that of our family
- We live longer than men. We need to provide more than them for old age
- Do not rely on the pension contributions made by our partners as they might not remain our partners in the decades to come - divorced women have much smaller pension pots than divorced men, and single mothers have the smallest pension pots of all
- Have honest discussions about who pays for what and why it is that women are far more likely to pay for childcare than men, reducing our ability to invest in our pensions
- As always, fill up the awareness/knowledge gap - educate ourselves so we can put our awareness and knowledge to work
- reframe how we conceptualise pensions from 'another bill' to investing in a 'financial freedom fund'
- Recognise that with employer and government contributions, investing in your pension today gives you (effectively) free money today
- Stop procrastinating
- Save up to the maximum possible in a tax efficient manner via your company pension schemes
- Check that your company has actually enrolled you as sometimes either through ignorance or willful ignorance they fail to do so. Women suffer disproportionately here
- Do not rely on the combination of employer pensions and the state pension to see you through in older age as both of these can be less than 100% guaranteed and can be hit by economic events, and might not provide enough even if they do work as planned
- If you are self employed, (or not) set up independent means of investing for your later life whether this be via the stock market, property, alternatives or ideally a combination of all three (we will look at different investing options in later chapters).
- Protect yourself from fraud. The Financial Conduct Authority (FCA) has a lot of information about pension fraud and offers a

pension scam quiz. It's a good resource and should be your first port of call if you are considering switching your pension

- See useful resources at the end of the book for impartial advice on pensions

Chapter Four: The language gap

Money talks, but not to us

There is a gap in the way that the money world speaks to men and women which damages our financial health

Where it comes from

What we can do about it

- Female financial empowerment is a new (and still incomplete) phenomenon

- In Jersey, a UK Crown dependency, women were not taxed as individuals until 2021. Prior to that, women's income had to be declared on their husband's tax return - so he knew exactly much we earned

- In the UK, a married woman was unable to open a bank account in her own name without her husband's signed authorisation until 1975

- Until 1982, a pub could legally refuse to serve a woman

- The corporate world has not fully awoken to women's financial enfranchisement

- Starling Bank reports that the tone used in promoting financial products to women is often "demeaning, condescending and dumbed down"

- 71% of female-centric articles urged women to search for vouchers when they want to spend and 65% urged women to 'regain control' and 'not splurge'

- Articles about men and investments show that 73% suggest not coupon cutting but investing in art, cars, wine and property

- Those setting the tone of the corporate world are overwhelmingly male. There are more CEOs named Peter leading top UK companies than female CEOs

- Women make up just around 17% of Financial Conduct Authority-approved individuals. This figure has remained stubbornly unchanged since 2005

- The failure of the corporate world to achieve greater diversity means it is leaving money on the table. Companies with executive committees more than 1/3rd female have net profit margins *over 10 times greater* than men only committees[86]

- Yet, despite this, 15% of FTSE companies have executive committees composed exclusively of men

- Financial writers and commentators in the media are overwhelmingly male

- Women are less financially literate than men and less confident when operating in the money world

We've seen this awareness/knowledge gap above, with regard to women investing less of their pensions than men who earn comparable amounts. We shall see through this book that in general, women are less financially literate than men. This occurs for many reasons, some of them structural - the financial world is overwhelmingly populated by men - some of them psychological - the legacy effect of unconscious biases and social conditioning - all of them perpetuated by a messaging gap, by the different ways in which the money world speaks to men vs women.

The language used is different. The images used are different. The messages both overt and subliminal are different. And these differences are damaging.

Starling Bank, set up and run by fintech Pioneer Anne Boden, commissioned two research reports. The first, in 2018[87], reported on the different language used in promoting financial products to men vs women. Researchers found that the tone used in talking to women is often "demeaning, condescending and dumbed down," as if content is being written for "little girls instead of grown-ass women who know their way around a tax return."

Conquerors vs splurgers

Researchers cite masculine stereotypes urging readers to "conquer" the financial environment, with proactive language such as "make money, impress, score and stash," instead of the "scrimping and saving" referenced in content for women. Researchers found that 71% of female-centric articles urged women to search for vouchers when they want to spend and 65% urged women to 'regain control' and 'not splurge.'

The report mentions typing "investment" into the search bar of women's magazines. What generally comes up are designer handbags and expensive coats. There is nothing wrong with investing in a designer handbag as an *alternative investment* and I cover that in later chapters but that's not what these articles mean. This is the age-old trope: clothe your body in *this*. Reap some kind of indefinable reward for the superficialities of garb.

Investors vs coupon clippers

By contrast, articles about men and investments show that 73% suggest not coupon cutting but investing in art, cars, wine and property, and in so doing boosting the male image and status. These ads also suggest ways in which men can protect their money in the event of a divorce, implying women are a predatory threat to their financial well-being.

What toxic messages this sends to both genders.

The images that spring, juxtaposed, to my own mind are the ads we've all seen that show men standing, feet splayed, on the teak deck of a speedboat, powering towards some exotic island while the woman stands at a kitchen island hugging a jam jar of coins.

In 2021 Starling Bank released another report[88] addressing the imagery used in financial advertising that reinforces the speedboat/jamjar analogy.

Researchers from Brunel University, analysing over 600 photographs, found that men and women were depicted very differently. Men were portrayed as in control of making financial decisions, whereas women were pictured grasping piggy banks and counting pennies. Men are mostly shown with notes (53% compared to 44%) whereas women are more likely to be pictured with coins, often pennies (25% compared to 13%).

The toxic moulding of perceptions

The advertising industry would not be worth $1.7 trillion globally[89] if it were not effective at moulding our perceptions and influencing our behaviour. Coupon clippers versus speedboat racers. These are the background images that can seep into our subconscious as well as our conscious minds, and into the subconscious and conscious minds of our daughters, and our sons too, distorting the belief systems of both. Is it not limiting on our girls and pressuring on our boys to suggest that one can never aspire to high financial attainment whereas the other is hardly a worthy member of their gender if they do not and cannot?

This *input* moulds our relationship to money and helps determine how we act around it, warping our *output*.

Why is this? Why are the attitudes of the last century still informing the language of money, perpetuating the different ways in which the money world speaks to the genders?

I think part of the answer is to be found in the fact that, in evolutionary terms, we can measure the span of time during which women have enjoyed a measure of financial empowerment in the blink of an eye. Society is not used to women having control of money or assets. And neither, in some ways, are we.

Historical note

In the UK, until the Amendment of The Married Woman's Property Act in 1882, thanks to a system known as couverture, married women had no independent legal identity separate from that of their husbands. Until that time, effectively, they and all that was theirs, belonged to their husbands. If I had written this book then, ownership of the copyright would pass to my husband.

After 1882, couverture was dead. Or was it...

It took until 1926 for women to be allowed to hold and dispose of property on the same terms as men.

And until relatively recently, married women still lost aspects of their independent financial identity and single women still needed the financial endorsement of their fathers. Sheena Fraser worked for a bank in the 1960s. Fraser says her staff current account was transferred to a joint account while she was on honeymoon.[90]

"It said 'Mr (my husband's name) and another' and they also changed my contract to temporary staff. I later realised I couldn't build up a credit rating of my own because I was the second person named on the account, as well as on rents, loans, mortgages and so on. So getting a credit card in my own name still eludes me."

The position of single women was also problematic. In 1971, 23 year old Christine Edwards tried to buy a moped to ride to work.

"There was one for sale at a local dealership - one where you pedaled before the engine kicked in. I had saved the 30% deposit and wanted a hire purchase agreement to cover the balance."

She hit a stumbling block when the salesman insisted Edwards' father sign the contract.[91]

"I explained my parents were divorced and I wasn't in contact with my father but they wouldn't change their minds. They refused to take my mother's signature," she says.[92]

As late as the 1970s, working women were routinely denied mortgages in their own right, or were granted them only with the signature of a male guarantor.[93]

In the United States until as recently as 1974, prior to the Equal Credit Opportunity Act, banks required divorced, widowed or single women to bring a man with them to cosign any application for credit, irrespective of their own income. And... The banks would discount the value of women's wages when calculating how much to lend them. *By up to 50%.*

What about one-dollar, one vote? This is what incomplete financial enfranchisement looks like.

Back to the UK. Not until the 1975 Sex Discrimination Act could married women open a bank account in their own names without their husbands' signed authorisation. But we still didn't have the full legal entitlement to spend our money as we chose. Until 1982, pubs were legally allowed to refuse to serve us.

And as for the tax man (almost certainly a man) married women did not exist as independent entities until 1990. Only then did we gain the right to be taxed as individuals. Prior to that our income had to be declared on our husband's tax return - so he knew exactly much we earned. In Jersey, a UK Crown dependency, that small freedom was not granted to women until 2021.

I rest my case.

What this historical note shows us is that until relatively recently, women did not have full agency in how we controlled, accessed or spent our money.

So it is not surprising that we do not feel fully financially enfranchised, and that neither do men consider us to be so. And the result is that many of us do not yet feel fully at home in this brave new world of money.

I suspect the belief systems generated by an absence of financial empowerment linger on intergenerationally in our unconscious biases.

And the reason this is so particularly damaging is that if we are not even conscious of this behaviour, we can't change it.

This is why Ann Boden's initiative of calling out this toxic gendered messaging is so important as it brings the biases to our consciousness and we can then attempt to change them. But I think there are other factors at work too:

1) Could it be that women are not sufficiently represented as corporate decision makers?
2) And could this also specifically be the case in the financial services industry?

The Peter Problem

To answer my first question, let me cite the **Women Count 2020** report by diversity and inclusion consultancy, the Pipeline. This reveals that as of 2021, there are more CEOs named Peter[94] leading top UK companies than female CEOs.[95]

The report also reveals that in the U.S. there are more Fortune 500 CEOs named John than female CEOs. The same tends to hold true for the Roberts, Jameses, Williams, and Michaels of this world.

Curing that, creating the conditions and the opportunities whereby women can flourish, can rise to the top of these companies, and wish to stay there, might just help change the language that is used to speak to women about money and financial products.

And from society's standpoint, creating these conditions would actually improve corporate profitability.

Why it pays to promote women

Companies with executive committees that are more than one third female have net profit margins *over 10 times greater* than men-only committees.[96] Yet, despite this, 15% of FTSE companies have executive committees composed exclusively of men.

This needs to change, for all our sakes.

Female representation in the money world

The Peter problem strikes again

Looking at the United Kingdom, in a 2021 sample of 253 fund managers, researchers found that there were more men called Richard, David, Nick or James than there were women.[97]

A study by the Financial Conduct Authority in November 2019[98], found that women make up just around 17% of Financial Conduct Authority-approved individuals. Despite several regime shifts, the FCA observes that this figure has remained remarkably and stubbornly unchanged since 2005[99].

Personal note

At least it's better than when I entered the corporate finance department of my US investment bank in 1985. I was the first executive woman they employed in the London office. It was a strange and inhospitable environment. I certainly felt like an outsider and for all the eight years that I worked for large investment banking institutions, I continued to feel like an outsider. That was one of the reasons I left. It was also rife with sexism and harassment, which I took for granted. It's now thanks to women of my daughter's generation that these practices have been called out as unacceptable.

Many of those with whom I worked now populate the Sunday Times Rich List. I'm very happy with the trade-offs I made. I'm very happy I left when I did and continued my professional roles in the financial world on my own terms and as an individual but I sincerely hope that the environment has become friendlier towards women in 2021. There are more women employed in that world today but still not nearly enough.

A report by career experts Zippia reveals that in the United States gender diversity in investment banking has remained remarkably stubborn too. If we look at the data below from 2008 till 2018 we see that the percentage of women employed as investment bankers has actually fallen slightly over that decade.

Investment Banker Gender Over Time

This data shows how men and women predominate in the investment banker position over time.

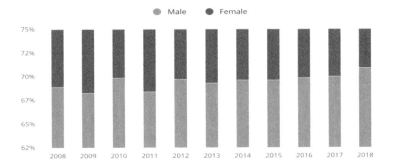

Source: Zippia https://www.zippia.com/investment-banker-jobs/demographics/

In the United States the voice of women in senior positions is scarcely loud enough to be registered.

Studies conducted by the Harvard Business School[100] reveal that in venture capital, private equity, and hedge funds women occupied just 9%, 6% and 11% of senior management roles. Of venture capital investors, that's the individuals who put their money where their mouth is and invest directly, only 8% are women, fewer than 1% are black.

The case for diversity

This matters for fairness, for inclusion, for social justice, but it also matters for profitability. Companies that are more homogenous are leaving money on the table. In the words of the authors of the report: "How do the financial outcomes of homogeneous partnerships compare with those of diverse collaborations? The difference is dramatic. Among all dimensions measured, the more similar the investment partners, the lower their investments' performance."

Money talks! Time for the corporate world to listen to a language that historically, it has always understood.

If we broaden our analysis to look at the financial services sector as a whole in the United Kingdom, as of 2018, a report by Statista.com[101] shows the mean weekly gross earnings for men was a whopping 54% higher than for women: £928 compared to £600.80. The data is not segregated into earnings differences for equivalent jobs but my hunch (which I'm fairly sure would be borne out by statistics) is that this is because women tend to fill the lower echelon positions while men will turn to be employed higher up the corporate structure, occupying the roles where decisions are made, where policy is crafted, where the language of money is formulated and spoken.

We've certainly seen that in the Peter Problem which afflicts the C-suite - Chief Financial Officer, Chief Executive Officer etc.

Progress

One piece of welcome good news and a real leap forward since I started writing *10 Things Everyone Needs to Know about Money* back in 2016 is the new and growing participation of women in hedge funds. A hedge fund is a pool of money that attempts to profit whether markets rise or fall. Hedge funds are among the most aggressive of investor types. Think Damian Lewis in *Billions*. But now they're not just Damians, there are Dianas too. When I asked a senior industry figure, Mark O'Hare of Preqin, in years gone by for data on women-run hedge funds, he said they had none because the number of women in hedge funds was vanishingly small, too small to be caught in the statistics.

Happily, that is changing. According to data from Preqin as of 2019,[102] 19.3% of hedge fund employees worldwide were women, up from 18.6% in 2017; 8.3% of board seats at hedge fund firms were held by women, up from 5.8% in 2017; and 11.2% of senior staff at hedge fund managers were women.

The Carmen portfolio

In what is either a shrewd commercial mood move, a canny marketing tactic, or probably a mix of the two, UBS has now launched a portfolio that invests exclusively in women-led hedge funds.[103] UBS has a database of more than 340 women who are either sole or joint managers of hedge funds or have significant influence over the decision-making of the fund.

UBS say this is an effort to improve diversity but also to find hidden talent in what has been a very male-dominated sector. They are calling this the *Carmen* portfolio. This is taking place against the backdrop of increased interest among the large institutional investor community in making investments on environmental social and governance grounds as well as investing performance.

Clearly both matter.

How are hedge funds run by women doing? The answer is that in the pandemic stock market plunge in spring of 2020 hedge funds run by women suffered lower losses than those run by men and they also did well in the bounce back. But in 2021, the first half they underperformed the general hedge fund index with the perception being they were protecting the downside rather more than profiting from the upside.[104]

Hopefully we will soon see even more female representation in hedge funds. Claire Tucker, the Senior Investment Officer at the UBS hedge fund unit, says that women have been "under represented particularly on the Investment side, despite a lack of evidence justifying that by skill or performance differences."[105]

The UK government appears to be aware of the widespread gender imbalance in the financial services industry and is attempting to redress this via its "Women in Finance Charter," which in their words is "a pledge for gender balance across financial services... It is a commitment by HM Treasury and signatory firms to work together to build a more balanced and fair industry. Firms that sign up to this Charter are pledging to be the best businesses in the sector.

The Charter reflects the government's aspiration to see gender balance at all levels across financial services firms. A balanced workforce is good for business.[106]

Fintech - financial technology

Fintech is the new, new thing and it has potential positive ramifications for women in the money world (we shall look at this in more detail when it comes to mortgage lending in a later chapter).

Anne Boden represents the cutting edge of fintech (financial technology) which is being rolled out across the financial services sector. She is a welcome but vanishingly rare voice.

A study by the Bank for International Settlements notes that "fintech promises to spur financial inclusion and close the gender gap in access to financial services." Hopefully it will do that but their own research paper published in March 2021 analysing 28 countries, finds a large 'fintech gender gap: while 29% of men use fintech products and services, only 21% of women do.'[107] They note that 'the gap is present in almost every country in our sample.'

Female financial advisors

How we can invest and how we can make our money work for us is something I will deal with in later chapters but it's worth touching on now Because this is another area where we are ill served. Only 15% of advisors are female, says Dr Ylva Baeckström, a lecturer in finance at Kings Business School in London.[108]

Baeckström says,[109] "Women are looking for advisors to understand them, who will not patronize them. That's not to say men won't fit the bill, but the way that the industry has traditionally offered advice has been in an alpha male way, which is not accessible. It's easier for a woman to feel more comfortable asking questions with a female advisor, who will be a woman who has made it in a man's world and understands all the language."

The (very few) women who speak money

Another side to this coin, is the paucity of female financial commentators. Female financial journalists and quoted female commentators are very much in the minority (as are female economists, a subject to which I shall return later.)

In recent years the Financial Times, edited by a woman but with a readership of only 20% women, conducted an analysis which shows that only 21% of people quoted in its pages were female. As a result it has developed a bot which analyses the gender of sources and alerts section editors if they're not featuring enough women.

This is a start, but we have a long way to go. The financial voice that speaks to us from the media is still overwhelmingly male. Women's voices in this domain are scarcely heard. Columnist and broadcaster, Grant Feller, in an excellent article entitled *It's none of your business, women,* wrote:

> Things have come far in the three decades I've been involved in journalism – but not in one crucial area. Business journalism. I recently wrote an article for the *British Journalism Review* about a typical week in British newspapers and how I discovered an astonishing imbalance between male and female writers. I counted 657 stories in the business pages, only 11 of which had a female writer's picture byline alongside it. The men had almost ten times as many – a pretty regular occurrence. But I think what has astonished me even more since it was published - and the BJR is a highly influential publication – is the almost total lack of interest in what I wrote about.

Source: https://journals.sagepub.com/doi/10.1177/0956474818798537

Why should more of us be reacting to this? It matters because the lack of female financial commentators will reinforce both conscious and unconscious biases about a woman's place in the financial world. About our authority within this world in the minds of readers both male and female.

It will make women feel less at home and the content itself, in terms of what is featured and how it is processed, will, certainly on occasion, have a gendered slant which speaks more to men and less to women.

For the sake of our authority and inclusion, we need more articles by women and more women to be quoted. We need to break this linguistic glass ceiling. We need to encourage more women to feel that this is a domain which we can enter and become part of. That this is a language we can speak, and that speaks to us. This in turn would create a virtuous circle rather than the current vicious one.

To sum up:

The money world speaks differently to men and women, with women being disadvantaged as a result. The reasons behind this are various. Some result from the fact that our financial enfranchisement is so recent. There are still intergenerational legacies holding us back and defining how we see ourselves in the money world and how the money world sees us. (I shall explore these psychological elements in the following chapters.)

Another major reason for these differences is the gender composition of the money world.

The financial world is remarkably homogeneous with little gender or ethnic diversity, especially at the higher levels. This sets the tone and perpetuates outmoded beliefs, practices and biases in the language of money. Decision makers' voices are far less likely to be female than male and it would be reasonable to suspect that might explain the differences in how these industries talk to men and women about money. And, crucially for us, how we respond.

This lack of diversity is undesirable in terms of social fairness and inclusion, but there is a further unwanted consequence that perhaps might be persuasive in moving that industry in the right direction. Research suggests that more diverse organisations are more profitable. It's not surprising that an echo chamber is created amongst homogeneous groups with consequent failure to conceive and capture a multitude of opportunities. Neither is it surprising that the echoes emanating from that chamber neither help, nor 'speak to' women. They would appear to be based on a spectrum of ideas that are at best outmoded and at worst plain insulting. The messages coming out of this financial world, the language and imagery used, are unappealing, excluding, disparaging and condescending towards women. They hold us back, help to create and perpetuate the financial literacy gap and damage our financial health.

It's entirely possible and indeed probable that those creating this language are not even consciously aware that they are doing so but are instead revealing the subconscious biases that they have inherited. Either way, the result is the creation of an effective linguistic and visual glass partition that keeps us in the financial waiting room. This is not helped by the paucity of female financial commentators and of female financial advisers. When the money world speaks, it speaks overwhelmingly with a male voice.

Wonderful initiatives such as Anne Boden's, (Anne being a stunning exception to the almost universal rule that it is men who set up and/or run financial services companies) have started the ball rolling.

Things are changing, female influence is percolating but profound change in the language used and those speaking it will I suspect take many years.

However, there is much that we can all do in the meantime.

What financial companies need to do:

- Examine how they market their services to men and women
- Examine both the overt and covert messages
- For everyone's sake, simplify the language used and avoid jargon
- Do a toxicity test before anything goes out under their name
- Be aware that women feel excluded
- Make efforts to counteract that and to make themselves more inclusive to women
- Solve the Peter problem. Aim for more diversity. Promote more women
- Improve your own profitability in doing so as well as striking a blow for social equity

What the media can do:

- Recruit and promote more female financial journalists
- Quote more female experts in the financial sphere
- Do its own toxicity test for the ads it carries and let advertisers know when they are shooting themselves in the foot with toxic messaging

What we can do:

- Do not judge your lack of fluency in the financial world
- That world is overwhelming male, and speaks with an overwhelmingly male voice which is notoriously bad at speaking to us
- It's only in very recent times that we have become fully financially enfranchised and that is still not the case for many women in many parts of the world
- Be aware that the intergenerational legacies of this lack of financial enfranchisement are likely to be lingering in your own unconscious biases (more of this later)
- Recognise that those same biases are rife in the money world itself
- Call them out when you see them
- Recognise how these biases get in the way of us making the best financial decisions for ourselves in the realm of borrowing, spending, saving and investing money (more on that later)
- Learn to spot the toxic messaging in financial advertisements
- Avoid the companies putting out toxic messaging and/or let them know how this is costing them your money vote
- Break the linguistic glass ceiling: learn to understand and speak the language of money. And make it work for you. This book is aimed at doing just that
- Increase your financial fluency by reading the finance and business pages in newspapers
- Have conversations with other women about money and finance
- Pick either a fiction or non-fiction book about money for your book club
- Read some financial thrillers to immerse yourself into that world in a fun way (see my own books which also have a heroine at the centre rather than merely as a love interest!)
- Talk to your children about money and the money world, particularly your daughters
- If we are sophisticated investors, ask our fund managers about female only funds. Check them out and if you think they're worth investing in, invest
- Look for female financial advisers (more of this later)
- Make Fintech your friend, as we shall see you later, Fintech while

it doesn't achieve gender neutrality, tends to be a lot less biased whether consciously or subconsciously, than human beings

Enough with languishing in the financial waiting room.

It is to borrowing that we now turn. Borrowing is such a huge topic that can have positive, negative, or a mix of both, effects on our financial health that it deserves three chapters to show the Good, the Bad and the Ugly.

Chapter Five: The bad side of debt

The gender debt gap:

We pay more than men to obtain debt

We get the worst kinds of debt pushed on us

We have less access to the good kinds of debt

There is a profound conflict of interest between us and the debt industry. We want to free ourselves, they want to hook us.

- Women have lower credit scores than men: 652 versus 702. The lower the credit score, the more expensive it is for us to borrow

- The cost of lifetime borrowing for women is nearly £17,000 more than for men - £152,403 compared with £135,49

- We are less likely to use products that help build our credit profile, such as personal loans, credit cards or mortgages

- But more likely to use ones that don't help us, like Buy Now Pay Later. 75% of BNPL users are female

- The over-indebted population is younger, more likely have children (58%), to live in private rented accommodation, and more likely to be female (55%)

- 37% of young women struggle to make cash last until the end of the month compared with 29% of young men in the same position

- A third of young mothers say they are permanently in debt

- In 2008 in the UK, the overall male insolvency rate was 56% higher than that for women. That flipped in 2014 and by 2018 the female rate of insolvency had become 14% higher than for men

- 61% of female victims of partner abuse have been coerced into debt by financial abuse

- 60% of payday loan borrowers are female

- Women are targeted for some of the most high risk debt specifically because of our gender

- Debt charity StepChange reports that around two-thirds of the 600,000 people a year who seek advice about problem debts are women and single mothers who find themselves compelled to borrow to **buy everyday necessities**

- One in two adults with debts has a mental health problem and one in four people with a mental health issue is also in debt

- In the UK, more than 100,000 people attempt suicide every year because of outstanding debts

- Out of 176 million credit card users in the United States, 45% of are *revolvers* - they carry a balance to the next month at least once every quarter

- Poverty is big business. Fringe financial services extract on average, $2500 in debt service from the 40 million households in the US with annual incomes under $30,000

- Debtors' prisons are no longer confined to the history books - 44% of Americans wouldn't have the money to cover a $400 fine – so many serve time in jail instead

- One third of US states now jail people for not paying their debts, even for minor infractions like traffic fines

Time to explore the multifaceted nature of debt: it can be good, bad and ugly; it can be different things to different genders. Women have more bad debt than men, we pay more for it than men, and men have more good debt than women.

Perhaps we should look upon debt like Janus, the two-faced god, the god of transitions and doors: not only can it be different things to different people, it can transport them to different places, some to a better place and some to a much worse place.

It's particularly imperative and timely that we understand more about debt as due to increasing inflation, debt will come knocking on more of our doors, kicking some of them down.

Inflation and debt

Inflation will have a negative double whammy on debt.[110] First of all it is responsible for a burgeoning cost of living crisis where increasing numbers of people will struggle to make ends meet. For some this will push them into debt, for others it will increase their reliance on debt. For everyone, it will increase the cost of debt as interest rates rise, putting a further squeeze on household finances.[111]

This will exaggerate the bad side of debt.

We are addicted to credit. The word sounds good, doesn't it? We speak of giving someone *credit*. We *credit* them with some kind of achievement. Debt sounds darker. We never think about how many *debt* cards we have, but that's the real question.

But it is we who suffer the consequences, not the debt-pushers.

Repayment of debt is freighted with moral judgements but those judgements are not today applied to the purveyors of debt, to the predatory lenders who push debt upon us, manipulatively and disproportionately targeting women. This is the truly ugly side of debt.

Hope vs desperation

Using debt is basically spending money we don't have based on an optimistic premise that we will have not just the same amount of money to repay in the future but *more* as we need to cover the interest burden of the debt as well. But it can also be taken out not on the basis of hope but of desperation. It would seem reasonable to assume that given the gaps described above women are going to be more susceptible to the necessity of debt than men because our income and pensions are typically less while things cost the same for us as they do for men, don't they?

Actually they often cost us more, thanks to the "pink premium." An analysis of hundreds of products by the Times[112] in 2016 found that where equivalent products were priced differently, they cost 37% more for women than equivalent items marketed at men and boys. The report states that many high street retailers were "often charging women up to twice as much as men for practically identical products." The "sexist" prices, particularly noticeable on such products as razors and pens, were found at many of Britain's biggest retailers, including Tesco, Boots and Amazon.

Nice bit of manipulative marketing. Slap on some pink paint and up your profit margin at our expense…

This manipulative marketing doesn't just apply to physical products, it also applies to the cost of debt itself. One of the gendered dimensions of debt we see in the UK (and in the US which I'll come to later) is that it costs women more than it does men.

Debt and the 'gender credit gap.'

This manifests in many ways, across all kinds of debt. We shall cover it across this and the next two chapters.

Women pay more to borrow than men

Credit Karma, a credit and financial management platform, reported [113] in a 2021 study reported that their female users have an average credit score of 652 compared to an average of 702 among their male customers. The lower the credit score, the more expensive it is for us to borrow. We get charged a higher rate of interest because we are perceived as riskier bets.

Credit Karma reported that the cost of lifetime borrowing for women was nearly £17,000 more than for men - £152,403 compared with £135,49.

I can already hear the chorus of objections: *credit karma indeed, it's your own responsibility, you need to accept that you are not as financially reliable as we men are, that you are a riskier bet.*

That might, on occasion, be *part* of the explanation but it in turn begs the question: *why* are we more financially precarious, and the answer to that as we shall see, is often a result of the patriarchal structures that we find ourselves living in with all the ramifications that affect our financial literacy and financial empowerment.

But there are other structural effects at work that have nothing to do with our financial probity but everything to do with how the money world operates and views us:

- We are less likely to use products that help build our credit profile,[114] such as personal loans, credit cards or mortgages
- Nearly a third of women (31%) have financial arrangements only in their husband's name and not in their joint names. This means, for debt history purposes, we are ghosts
- Sometimes even when debt is in the joint names of husband and wife, if the woman's name comes after the name of her male partner, it has less of a positive impact on her credit scores

The Credit Karma report cited above has some useful tips which it argues will make women more appealing to lenders:

1. Have a mobile phone contract or a credit card in your name.
2. Pay your bills on time.
3. Get on the electoral roll. This provides proof of address and that you have stable living arrangements.

Interestingly, what we do use more is Buy Now Pay Later "BNPL" schemes. A government report published in 2021[115] shows that 75% of BNPL users are female.

There are various problems with BNPL which I explore in depth in a later chapter but one problem relevant here is that BNPL services do not have a positive effect on our credit scores although as we shall see, they can have a negative impact.

Women have a greater need of debt and are more likely to develop problems with debt than men

Over-indebtedness, borrowing more than you can afford to repay, or at a level whereby repayments force you into penury, is a growing problem globally and across genders, but it is more acute for women.

In 2017, UK households' outgoings exceeded their income for the first time since 1988, with debt filling the gap according to a report by the Women's Budget Group.[116] The ever more frequent use of debt to make ends meet has become a way of life, particularly for the poorer sections of society globally, which means, disproportionately, for women. In 2019, UK Households collectively owed £1.6 trillion, 13% higher than at the time of the 2008 Global Financial Crisis.[117] In 2018, pre-Covid, 1 in 6 individuals in the UK were over-indebted, 8.2 million in total. The over-indebted population is younger, more likely have children (58%), to live in private rented accommodation, and more likely to be female (55%).[118]

The Young Women's Trust in a November 2020 report found that 37 per cent of young women struggle to make cash last until the end of the month compared with 29 per cent of young men in the same position.

If we turn to India, a study by Isabelle Guérin & Christophe Nordman & Elena Reboul,[119] finds that women there are heavily indebted, borrowing much more than men relative to their income. The authors report that: "female debt is predominantly - and markedly more than male – used to make ends meet, while productive investment remains in great part a male privilege. Last, it is in the poorest and the lowest caste households that women manage the highest shares of household debt."

They conclude that:

"From a theoretical perspective, these results underline the gender earmarking of debt and credit, i.e. the fact that male and female debt/credit do not have the same meaning and use."

Janus has many faces...

Turning back to the United Kingdom we see that, as from 2014, women are more likely than men to suffer from problem debts which end in insolvency. This is the progression of a trend that began years earlier. A report by the job site for the over 50's, Rest Less[120] showed that in 2008 in the UK, the overall male insolvency rate was 56% higher than that for women. That flipped in 2014 and by 2018 the female rate of insolvency had become 14% higher than for men.

The number of insolvencies amongst women increased significantly in every age group between 2008 and 2018, with more women being bankrupt then men in the 25 to 34 age cohort, but the jump was biggest amongst the over 65s (88%) followed by women aged between 45-54 (69%) and the over 55s more generally (69%).

This trend has seen the number of women over 65 entering insolvency nearly doubling over 10 years.[121]

Why are women developing more problem debts than men?

It would appear that women are finding it more difficult than men to make ends meet. Debt charity StepChange reports that around two-thirds of the 600,000 people a year who seek advice about problem debts are women and single mothers who find themselves compelled to borrow to **buy everyday necessities**. Because of inflation these trends will worsen. StepChange estimates that 20% of Brits are expected to fall into "problem debt" in 2022.

The debt consequence of economic abuse

Women can also become indebted because of economic abuse. In a survey of female victims of intimate partner abuse, 61% reported that they were in debt as a result of financial abuse.[122] Research in the United States also cites how women in abusive relationships may end up with high levels of "coerced debt," which can lead to poor credit ratings, which will increase the cost of borrowing, on top of the legacy debt taken on as a result of the coercive control, further undermining her financial health.[123] This is a subject to which we shall return in chapter 11.

Another reason that women are more likely than men to end up

insolvent is that we are more likely than men to have to make use of one of the most damaging kinds of loans - payday loans.

Studies show that a disproportionate percentage of payday loan borrowers are female.[124]

Payday loans, predatory lending and women

Payday loans are particularly damaging because of the super-high interest rates which compound into exponentially increasing debt burdens and because of the lack of financial resilience of those most likely to take them out.

This type of debt is taken out as an act of desperation by people with very few options and minuscule or non-existent reserves, typically amongst the most vulnerable people in our societies worldwide.

Payday loans are emergency loans almost invariably borrowed when something has gone wrong, where there has been some unforeseen expense that cannot be met from savings. This could be a car irretrievably breaking down, your roof springing a leak, the fridge packing up during a heatwave, a family member amassing gambling debts, or parking fines.

Women are more likely than men to take out payday loans and can be targeted specifically because of our gender.

In the United States, a 2010 study[125] analysing visitors to eighteen different internet payday loan sites found that 64% were women. Over half of those women had children. The suggestion is that a significant portion of these borrowers were single mothers. A different study[126] using 2007 Federal Reserve data also found that a disproportionate number of female-headed households were using payday loans, compared to households headed by men or married couples.

The preponderance of female payday loan customers is replicated internationally.

A recent study by the Financial Conduct Authority in the UK in 2019 found that 60% of payday loan borrowers were female.[127] An earlier report showing 25% more women than men use payday loans in the UK, suggests that this is partially a result of manipulative marketing that specifically targets women, marketing which glamorises payday loans and offers them as a **lifestyle accessory rather than an emergency solution to a desperate problem.**[128]

Predatory Lending

Like the predatory lenders who sold mortgages to people way beyond their ability to ever repay them, ultimately causing them to lose their homes,[129] payday loan lenders also have been guilty of predatory lending: lending to people who never have a hope of repaying. We examine this with regard to mortgage lending later.

Bad and ugly - how payday loans operate

These loans are meant to be a short-term solution to acute financial problems. They are meant to be repaid when your wages or salary fall into your account at the end of the month.

However, the solution they offer very often turns out into a far bigger problem.

The reality is with all payday loans, unless you repay them in full from your next paycheck, you are in all likelihood going to struggle to repay them at all due to the egregiously high rates of interest and the massive compounding effect of unpaid loans.

Let me give you an example, along with the maths. Let's say your car breaks down and you need it to get to work because you work unsociable hours and public transport at that time is not safe or available and you also need to drive your kids to school because you don't live on a public transport route. The long and the short of it is you have to buy a car. So you go to a payday loan lender and you borrow £1000.

You reckon you can pay it off when your salary drops into your bank account next month and the following month.

I just googled payday loans on finder.com. Many of them offer a fixed interest rate equivalent to 292% per annum.[130]

However as is often the case with anything to do with money, it's not as simple as that and you might well end up paying far, far higher rates of interest than that (although that is bad enough as we see below).

When you look at the APR (annual percentage rate) which takes into account fees charged for providing the loan, and the compounding effects of non-repayment (where you end up paying interest on interest), the effective interest rate goes up to over a thousand percent in almost all cases and in one case, to a whopping 1427%.

The maths

An interest rate of 292% per annum is equivalent to 24.3% per month. At the end of one month, you would incur an interest payment of £243. It's easy to calculate this. If you have an iPhone have a look at the Utilities function and go on the calculator. Input 24.3 (or whatever interest rate is being offered for the month) then hit %, then X 1000 (or whatever value of loan you're seeking to take out) then hit = to give you the cost of the first batch of interest.

If you don't pay that interest and repay the loan in full there and then, you must add that interest to the principal, and then the next batch of interest is calculated on £1243, which equals £302.

If you pay that back at the end of two months you will have paid back **£545** of interest and **£1000** of principal.

If however you have a problem and you have to roll the loan over then it quickly begins to snowball.

If you roll it over and repay it at the end of six months, you will end up paying **£2687** in interest and the **£1000** principal.

If you have to roll it over for the entire year, at the end of 12 months, the total you will need to repay will be **£13,597**, i.e. **£12,597** of interest and the **£1000** of principal repayment, see below. This equates to an annual effective interest rate of *1260%*.

Time since loan	Principal	Interest	Principal plus interest
1 month	1000	243	1243
2 months	1243	302	1545
3 months	1545	375	1920
4 months	1920	467	2387
5 months	2387	580	2967
6 months	2967	720	3687
7 months	3687	896	4583
8 months	4583	1114	5697
9 months	5697	1384	7081
10 months	7081	1721	8801
11 months	8801	2139	10939
12 months	10939	2658	13597

You borrow £1000 and you end up repaying £13,597. And who if they are desperate to get their hands on £1000 can ever hope to find £13,597? The bailiffs would come in and bankruptcy threaten.

This is why payday loans are so pernicious. If you cannot repay within a short space of time, your loan will increase at a faster rate than ever your salary or wages could hope to do. When you're on that treadmill as many have found, it's almost impossible to get off. The consequences can be catastrophic.

So why do people take them out?

Desperation combined with poor financial literacy

The 2019 study by the FCA, quoted above, reports that 61% of consumers with a payday loan have low confidence in managing their money, compared with 24% of all UK adults. In addition, 56% of consumers with a payday loan rated themselves as having low levels of knowledge about financial matters. These compare with 46% of all UK adults reporting similar levels of knowledge about financial matters. An earlier study in the US by the National Bureau of Economic Research in 2013[131] notes that "it is not only the shocks inflicted by the financial crisis or the structure of the financial system but that the level of financial literacy also plays a role in explaining why so many individuals have made use of high-cost borrowing methods."

We cannot undo the financial crisis and its consequences but we can improve financial literacy.

This is particularly essential now in this inflationary era Where more people are going to be falling into debt traps. However, if you think payday loans are bad, they pale in comparison to 'loan sharks' - illegal money lenders who charge much higher rates of Interest than the already egregious levels charged by payday loan lenders and often resort to violence and theft to get repaid.

The Centre for Social Justice estimates that more than two million people are already in debt to illegal money lenders.[132] And to make matters worse, it is the poorest, most vulnerable members of society who are most at risk of falling victim to illegal loan sharks.

The ensnaring. Debt is big business and the product is... You

Time to take a look at the face of the money lenders, the creditocracy. In this section I will expose one of the business models that consumes us, so that we can better recognise it, resist it, and fight back against it.

The creditors, aka the moneylenders

Throughout history, lending money has been a contentious, morally freighted issue. We have Shylock in the Merchant of Venice (*if you cut me, do I not bleed?*) appealing to our shared humanity so we might see him as human despite him being a much-hated moneylender. We saw the murders and pogroms of the moneylenders by those who wished to see their debts die along with their creditors. We saw temple loans made on behalf of ancient gods with those ancient gods as the creditor (the debtors tended to repay!). We have Aristotle cursing the lending of money as *barren, unnatural and hated*. We have old prohibitions against usury, in Judaism, Islam and Christianity.[133]

So, while lending money has historically had a bad rep, the moneylenders of today are cannier. They dress it up, they make it look as if they are doing us a great service, a favour, making our life easier.

They make it look as if we are in control but the reality is, we are being played. Moneylending is big business and it's getting ever bigger. We are the product, very often the prey.

We, the consumers of debt, often end up being consumed by it.

Most lenders need not and often do not have our best interests at heart. (Please see my last book, *10 Things Everyone Needs To Know About Money*, where I write extensively about this.[134]) Very often *they don't even care whether you will be able to repay the money*, whether the loan they are offering you will bankrupt you, or as is often the case in the United States, see you sent to prison (recreating effective debtors prisons).

The Creditocracy

Institutionalising debt, *domesticating* debt until it becomes a permanent fixture in daily life, is the reality of the creditocracy.[135] It is profitable for the providers of credit to keep us on the hook. It is profitable for a capitalistic society to encourage us to keep on wanting more and more stuff, often stuff that we cannot afford, do not need, which does not make us happier and degrades the planet in the process of its extraction and subsequent disposal.

Almost at every turn, credit is being pushed at us from seemingly respectable sites that fuel consumerism. Maybe in the absence of spirituality there is only 'stuff.'

Profiting from poverty

Poverty is big business. Gary Rivlin in his book *Broke USA. From pawnshop to poverty,*[136] writes how the world's working poor have become big business. He says that "taken as an industry average, fringe financial services collectively extract $2500 in debt service from each of the 40 million households in the US with incomes of less than $30,000 per annum – equivalent to a 10% property tax."[137]

Rivlin estimates that $30 billion in fees and interest payments is extracted in this way.

And extracted it is, one way or another, as millions of people simply cannot pay and are captured in a debt trap.

77 million Americans have a debt that has been turned over to a debt collection agency.[138]

In the UK, a study by the Young Women's Trust, published in November 2020[139] found that almost 40% of young women struggle to make their cash last until the end of the month and a third of young mothers say they are permanently in debt.

Young women and the debt trap

One in three of the women surveyed above, said they did not expect to be able to escape the debt trap until over 40.

This report linked young women's experience of debt with:

1) **Pay inequality**: over one in five young mothers reported being paid less than the minimum wage and less than male colleagues doing the same or similar work

2) **Unaffordable childcare**: a third of young mothers report turning down or leaving work because they couldn't afford childcare
3) A **complex benefit system** and **sexism**

The consequences of problem debt:

1) Mental health

The Royal College of Psychiatrists notes that "debt can cause - and be caused by - mental health problems." They estimate that one in two adults with debts has a mental health problem and one in four people with a mental health issue is also in debt.[140]

They go on to note that how debt makes people feel depressed, anxious, guilty, hopeless, embarrassed to discuss their financial situation, and feel like everything is out of control, and that creditors can behave in "inappropriate" and sometimes "distressing" ways when attempting to recover debts.

More than 100,000 people attempt suicide every year because of outstanding arrears, a report by the Money and Mental Health Policy Institute estimated in December 2020.[141]

The problem is made worse by the taboo around money in general and around money problems in particular. Breaking the taboo and talking to people is essential. There are various resources and organisations that can help us with problem debt - see data resources at the back of the book.

2) Debtors' prisons

These are the stuff of nightmares, of Dickens and Hogarth, of mother's ruin and despair.

The stuff of history you might say.

The practice of jailing people for unpaid debts ebbed away in the United Kingdom in the 1900s and was formerly outlawed in the United States in the 1833[142] and yet... In the US if you fall into arrears and if civil debt proceedings are initiated against you, if the judge considers that you *wilfully declined to appear and that you are wilfully avoiding repaying your debt,*[143] you can be, and often are, sent to jail.

 A BBC report in April 2018 stated that "nearly 44% of Americans wouldn't have the money to cover a $400 fine" – so thousands serve time in jail instead.[144]

This impacts Black and Latino communities disproportionately as a result of intergenerational racial and ethnic gaps in wealth and poverty. Gendered data is not available but I would hazard a guess that women, particularly women of colour, and single mothers, who are caught most fixedly in the poverty trap, suffer disproportionately as they experience both racial economic inequality and gender economic inequality.[145]

One third of US states now jail people for not paying their debts, even for minor infractions like traffic fines. Some apply surcharge collection fees and additional "poverty penalties" through the court system. These states are effectively monetising people's poverty for their own municipal benefit. Elizabeth Patterson[146] who has campaigned extensively on the subject, says that local governments "rely on the revenue generated by these fees." So much for justice being impartial...

Welcome to the world of moral hazard: a world where one party has an interest in an action that will damage the other party but in no way shares their pain.

The business model of many lenders is predicated on keeping you, the product, perpetually in a state of debt.

This is highly profitable as long as you have to keep paying it off, as long as you have the wherewithal to keep paying it off. Like a virus, or a parasite. It doesn't want to kill the host, it just wants to be there forever, sucking as much of your lifeblood as it can without killing you.

Out of 176 million credit card users in the United States,[147] 40.3% of are *revolvers* - they carry a balance to the next month at least once every quarter.[148]

Credit card debt companies however, are, as the financial world would have it, having their lunch eaten by the new game in town - Buy Now Pay Later - which we shall turn to in a subsequent chapter.

To sum up

Women have been on the wrong side of the debt equation throughout history. We consistently pay more for debt, have a greater need for debt to make ends meet and are more likely to suffer from problem debt than men. We have been targeted specifically because of our gender with particularly pernicious and damaging types of debt. Many of us are trapped in a perpetual cycle of debt. In the United States, we can end up in prison if we are unable to pay our debts.

There is a fundamental conflict of interest between us and the debt industry. We want to pay off all debts, freeing ourselves of the debt burden, they want to keep us in perpetual debt servitude so they might perpetually profit from it. Inflation and the burgeoning cost of living crisis it is causing, will increase the cost of servicing debt, necessitate more borrowing to make ends meet, expose more people to debt, and also to the worst kinds of debt - payday loan lenders and worst of all, illegal loan sharks.

What the government needs to do:

Re the UK, I'm going to paraphrase the Financial Conduct Authority[149] as it sets out what needs to be done very cogently:

- Create /encourage /sponsor more benign alternatives to high-cost credit
- The FCA should work with the Government and Bank of England to reform the regulation of credit unions and Community Development Finance Institutions
- More should be done to encourage mainstream lenders into this space
- Address the real world costs of ugly debt
- Frame regulation with a view to the outcome being sought and how consumers use products in the real world
- Regulation should deliver similar protections where consumers face similar harms
- In addition to making sure products are affordable, there should be an increased focus on lenders meeting consumers needs' for as long as they hold the product

- The FCA should review repeat lending

To this I would add:

- Focusing is all very well but you need teeth to redress the conduct of exploitative lenders
- Those exploited need greater protection, strong viable alternatives, and justice and compensation when exploited
- More should be done to shut down and prosecute illegal loan sharks
- And to raise awareness of what they are and how to avoid them

In the US, government needs to:

- Do all of the above, and
- Stop sending people to jail for non-payment of loans! Apart from the social damage done, how can they ever repay a loan when they are inside?
- Stop allowing states/municipalities to monetise poverty in this way for their own benefit

What companies need to do:

- Conduct a ruthless audit of your entire business model and ethics of it
- Try to be a provider of a worthwhile service rather than a corporate virus infecting your customers/victims
- Stop mis-selling payday loans
- Stop targeting whoever you feel is the least sophisticated and most vulnerable
- Stop pushing toxic product on them
- In marketing payday loans to show their true cost and potential cost and consequences
- Issue a visible and powerful health warning about their use
- Review the eligibility of borrowers much more carefully

What we can do:

- Learn to recognise and arm yourself against the ugly face of debt
- Factor in the risk and likelihood that further rises in inflation will lead to further rises in interest rates which will further increase the cost of current and future borrowings
- Educate yourselves and your families to fully understand the nature of debt and how the debt industry /creditocracy works
- Understand the fundamental conflict of interest between ourselves and lenders - they want us to remain perpetually in debt, we yearn to be debt free
- Recognise the power of and damage done by the creditocracy which attempts to normalise the use of debt
- See how the creditocracy regularly manipulates us into taking on debt (more on this later)
- Know that the debt industry will sometimes target us specifically because we are women and they consider us less financially aware than men
- Spot how and when they charge us more for debt than is appropriate (more on this later)
- Call them out! Take your business elsewhere or, if possible, don't borrow
- Refuse to be an easy mark for the creditocracy
- Avoid debt traps such as payday loans like the plague
- Do the maths! Understand the toxic side of compounding where money borrowed snowballs out of control
- Wherever humanly possible, save up a rainy day fund and keep it for emergencies
- If you have to deploy some or all of this fund, begin replenishing it as soon as possible
- Be aware of how the debt products you use can either help your credit profile or hinder it
- If taking on joint debt with your partner, examine how that can affect your credit rating depending on if you are named and in which order
- Forewarn yourself - debt is pushed on us from all sides and can sometimes be an impulsive decision
- Protect your resilience and your financial health - debt might seem like a good decision today but tomorrow we will pay for it in

more ways than one
- Be aware of the increasing numbers of women, especially older women, who become unable to bear the burdens of their debts and go insolvent
- Recognise that taking on debt and bearing the burden of debt can damage our mental health
- Pause long and hard before taking on debt
- Ask: do I really need this debt?
- Do I really need to buy what this debt facilitates?
- Is there a better way I can finance this if it buying/paying for it is truly essential?
- Recognise that coerced debt can be be a form of a form of domestic abuse which often goes hand in hand with domestic violence
- Seek help if you have been/or suspect you might have been coerced into debt either knowingly or unknowingly
- Recognise problem debts often go hand in hand with addiction and excessive spending can be a form of addiction in itself. Seek help, whether for yourself or a family member or friend who is/or could be affected.
- See useful resources at the end of the book for help with coerced and other kinds of problem debt

That is the ugly side of debt. In the next chapter we turn to the good side of debt, but see that even here, bad and ugly sides can lie hidden.

Chapter Six: The good side of debt

Which also has elements of the bad and ugly...

- Women profit less than men from the benefits and the wealth accumulation that debt can create

- While paying more for the privilege and carrying the burden of debt for longer than men

- And being at greater risk of default

- Mortgages

- When buying a home in England, women need over twelve times their annual salaries while men need just over eight times

- 10% of single women in the UK have mortgages compared to 17% of single men

- In 2016 in England the percentage of single male first time buyers was 17.7%, compared with 7.8% of single women

- But... In the US despite the fact that women earn, on average, only 84 cents for every male dollar earned, 19% of home buyers in 2019 were single females while only 9% were single males During the housing boom in the early 2000's in the US, men obtained more attractive mortgages than women, and lenders steered minorities and women toward subprime and less-desirable loan products, **even when they could have qualified for prime mortgages**

- The advent and increasing adoption of algorithmic machine based mortgage lending in the US (care of Fintech) has dramatically reduced discrimination in the granting and pricing of mortgages which benefits women and minorities

- Student debt

- In the UK, female graduates carry the burden of student debt for fourteen years while their male counterparts carry it for only eleven years

- Female graduates benefit less financially from their university education - starting salaries are £2,140 less than that of male graduates

- In the US, in 2016, while women account for 56% of undergraduates they hold almost 66% of total student debt. Their average debt on graduation is $2,700 greater than that of men

- 77% of black students took out a federal loan to pay for higher education compared to 60% of all students. And the average debt on graduation in 2012 was $29,344 for black students compared to a national average of $25,640.

- White women borrowed $31,346, on average, to fund undergraduate degrees. Black women borrowed $37,558.

- Venture capital

- Less than 1% of total UK venture capital goes to female founded companies. Male founders get 89 per cent and mixed-gender teams get 10%

- 83% of deals that UK VCs made last year had no women at all on the founding teams.

- At the current rate of glacial progress, for all-female teams to reach even 10% of all deals will take until 2045

- Yet the industry is leaving money on the table again! The financial returns on investing in women are more than twice as much per dollar invested, as those on investing in men.

We looked at some of the ugly faces of debt above. Now it is time to turn to some of the potentially pleasant aspects. Yet even they have different faces: good and bad.

Let's take a look at three kinds of debt we typically take out in a spirit of optimism, not desperation:

- Mortgages
- Student loans
- Borrowing to fund the creation or expansion of a business

We shall see below that all three of these have a gender dimension where, on average:

- Women profit less than men from the benefits and the wealth accumulation that debt can create
- While paying more for the privilege
- Carrying the burden of debt for longer than men
- And being at greater risk of default

The golden passport

How many of us would have been able to buy a home without the golden passport provided to us by mortgage debt?

This golden passport offers us a kind of time travel whereby we get to occupy and enjoy our home today, while saving up for it might have taken us 30 years. Plus, by the time we had saved enough the price would have moved again beyond our reach, so we would never have been able to afford it without debt.

Home ownership and the gender gaps

Owning your own home, having a roof over our head where we feel safe is right up there in the hierarchy of human needs. Ok, you could argue that renting a home will fulfill the same basic functions of security and safety but I would dispute this. Home ownership is one of the most fundamental ways in which we can create long-term wealth and financial security for ourselves because we are not exposed to the vagaries of the rental market but also because property consistently goes up in value over time. If we are able to keep up our mortgage payments then one day our home will be freely ours to enjoy on multiple levels. Rent, as anyone who has ever rented knows too well, just disappears and we have nothing to show for it. The implications for wealth creation and providing for ourselves in our old age are enormous:

A study by the Federal Reserve[150] found that in 2019, homeowners in the U.S. had a median net worth of $255,000, while renters had a net worth of just $6,300.

As well as being a haven, our home is a financial asset that if we need to liquidate, to downsize, we can free up capital in older years if needed. On top of this, our home as haven provides powerful psychological benefits which can be fundamental to our mental and physical health. It gives us a feeling of safety, of refuge.

Owning a home is, I get it, a privilege and a boon. For those of us lucky enough to be able to obtain a mortgage, investing in property has been a good financial decision as well as a means of providing us with a home. In *10 Things Everyone Needs to Know about Money* I write extensively about the benefits of ownership. It's no secret. The secret is finding out how on earth we can amass sufficient funds to put down a deposit and access a mortgage given the dwindling supply.

Is home ownership equally available to women and men?

I analysed data in the United Kingdom and the United States and got some surprising answers. *No* in the United Kingdom, *yes* in the United States.

Let's dig deeper:

UK - More single men are buying homes than single women. Given the gender pay gap, that is no surprise.

10% of single women in the UK have mortgages compared to 17% of single men according to a survey by RealHomes.[151]

Another report by Statista, analysing data over the period 2015 to 2016 in England alone showed that the percentage of single male first time buyers was 17.7%, compared with 7.8% of single women.

A report compiled by the Women's Budget Group in 2019 suggests why this might be the case. Here again we see the consequences of the gender pay gap: **when buying a home in England, women need over twelve**

times their annual salaries while men need just over eight times.[152]

The same report shows that average rents in England take 43% of women's median earnings compared to 28% of men's, and that there are now no regions in England where the average home to rent is affordable for a woman on median earnings.

Among men, the average home to rent is affordable in every region except London and the southeast.

The implication is that as a woman, if you want to own or rent a property, you need to do so as part of a couple and a heterosexual couple at that, unless you have access to inheritance or parental support. Having a great education and working hard is often not enough. Women who aren't in a relationship, or have exited one, or who wish to but cannot find a home to go to, are likely to struggle.

"This report highlights the link between providing women with safe, secure, good quality, affordable accommodation and the wider fight for women's equality," says Denise Fowler, chief executive of Women's Pioneer Housing and co-chair of the Women's Housing Forum.[153] As she observes:

"Without a safe, secure, affordable home of her own, no woman can achieve her potential. I hope it will be a call to action across the UK."

There is another reason however that might be holding us back - confidence and the legacy effect of financial disenfranchisement.

The financial literacy paradox

We women are actually more financially literate than we realise but a lack of confidence and self belief is holding us back. A 2019 survey[154] **by the Homeowners Alliance reports notes:**

"Another hurdle women face on the road to owning their own home is having the confidence to find the best mortgage product. We've found that men are far more confident about their mortgage understanding. In a survey we asked men and women to tell us if they understood a mortgage term, then asked them to define it. A higher percentage of men said they understood terms than women. But when asked to actually explain what the term meant women had a similar or better knowledge than men." Sound familiar?

Being financially literate by itself is not enough. When we are, we need to *believe* it!

And before you think this is a criticism of women, or a mindless exhortation to: *Go Girl!* - it is absolutely not. The legacy effect of generations of women feeling they did not have a place in the Money World, did not understand it, didn't actually belong there is at work here.

It's not remotely surprising that we are not confident in the Money World as it has been deeply inhospitable to us for millennia, and even when the law has allowed us to step into it, that world has not spoken to us and engaged with us in a way that is likely to make us feel comfortable and confident (see Ann Boden's *Make Money Equal* campaigns).

The Money World itself needs to change, to make itself more hospitable to us so that we can engage progressively more with it in a virtuous circle and in so doing become more comfortable and confident.

And, in the United States, the Money World is changing, thanks to a stunning, machine-based financial innovation which is having dramatic effects on women's financial enfranchisement and health.

The United States - More single women are buying homes than single men, despite the existence of a pay gap.

Despite the fact that women earn, on average, only 84 cents for every male dollar earned,[155] 19% of home buyers in 2019 were single females while only 9% were single males.[156]

Why is this? Why are US women so much keener and /or more able than men to get on the housing ladder?

The answer would seem to be part psychological and part due to structural financial innovation.

Psychological - A 2018 report by Bank of America found that 73% of women value home ownership above getting married and having children, compared with 65% of men.

Structural - Thanks to the rise of digital lending technology, the prejudices and biases that have got in our way in the past are no longer obstructing us to the same extent. Both gender and racial prejudice in the mortgage sector is decreasing.

The role of the mortgage lender sitting in their office deciding to grant or not to grant mortgages, and how to price those mortgages, acting on conscious or unconscious bias, is in decline.

A report by the National Bureau of Economic Research in 2019[157] suggest that digital algorithmic based mortgage lenders discriminate about 40% less than traditional mortgage companies, approving more loans to women and minorities and at a lower cost. The authors state that "FinTech algorithms have not removed discrimination, but two silver linings emerge. Algorithmic lending seems to have increased competition or encouraged more shopping with the ease of applications. Also, while face-to-face lenders discriminate against minorities in application rejection, there are reasons to believe FinTechs may discriminate less."

It's interesting to note the authors comments that the algorithms have not removed *all* discrimination. The algorithms are, of course, based on formulae and weightings entered into them and created by human beings, but in doing so these individuals will be confronted by any conscious prejudices and biases that they have and will have an opportunity to remove those biases. What remains will be their unconscious biases.

These automated lenders are also reducing gender and racial discrimination in the pricing of mortgages.

The report found that black and Latino homebuyers currently pay an interest rate that's 0.079% higher on average than other borrowers amounting to about $765 million in additional interest per year as a result.

The same report notes that algorithmic lending also reduces discriminatory decisions to accept or reject a mortgage application. In face to face mortgage application process, Black and Latinx borrowers are rejected 6% more than non-minority ones, *even when they have the same financial profiles*. The study found that automated mortgage solutions would have removed this bias, treating comparable candidates equally.

A report released in 2020 by Compass and digital mortgage lender Better.com reinforces these findings. Over the course of 2019, the company saw the number of single, minority female borrowers using its algorithm-based lending platform increase by 500%, with the number of single women borrowers in the 30-to-40 age range rising by 450%.[158]

Nearly 25% of their borrowers were single females compared to an industry average of 17%.[159]

The advent of digital mortgage lending platforms is especially welcome when we look at the history of mortgage lending in the United States, specifically with reference to the subprime era in the 2000s where women and minorities were actively discriminated against.

Historical note

Studies of the subprime mortgage crisis which brewed up in the 2000's and brought the world to its knees financially in 2007-2008 reveal that men obtained more attractive mortgages than women, and that lenders steered minorities and women toward subprime and less-desirable loan products, even when they could have qualified for prime mortgages.[160]

Women earning double the median income were 46.4% more likely to receive subprime mortgages than men in that income cohort. This disparity was particularly marked in women of colour. Upper income African American women were nearly five times more likely and Latino women four times more likely to receive subprime purchase mortgages than white men in the same income bracket.[161]

There is double discrimination with women being more likely to receive subprime mortgages than men of the same race. African American women were 5.7 percent more likely than African American men to receive subprime mortgages; Latino women were 12.7 percent more likely than Latino men to receive subprime mortgages; and white women were 25.8 percent more likely to receive subprime purchase mortgages than white men.

Single women also suffered. Amy Castro Baker in her 2014 paper, Eroding the wealth of women: gender and the sub-prime foreclosure crisis,[162] observes that "the overrepresentation of single women in the sub-prime lending pool cannot be explained by assets, property location, or market conditions.[163] Rather, they were targeted."[164]

As were women in general, women of colour, and single women, all of whom were more likely to take-up subprime loans than men, even when they would have qualified for prime mortgage loans.

This was the work of predatory lenders.

Predatory loans involve "engaging in deception or fraud, manipulating the borrower through aggressive sales tactics, or taking an unfair advantage of a borrower's lack of understanding about loan terms."[165]

The predatory loan market is typified by lenders shopping for customers rather than the other way around. The lenders solicit the borrowers. They target particular neighbourhoods and demographic groups, often going door-to-door, particularly in neighbourhoods of colour.

Apart from the shocking iniquities of these findings, the inequalities, the prejudices which are implicit, the consequences are enormous. Subprime borrowing costs more, reduces borrowers' ability to save and accordingly increases their vulnerability to any kind of financial shock. Specifically it increases the risk of default, repossession and eviction.

That is why the advent of algorithmic digital lending programs is so particularly welcome. But predatory lenders and subprime loans persist and the best way to protect people and communities against them is financial education.

Owning property is one of the key determinants of wealth creation and preservation. If you cannot afford to buy property or if you end up paying more for the privilege than you need to, your ability to create wealth will be severely hampered, as a disproportionate amount of women know to their cost.

Student debt

If we turn our attention to student debt, we can see again the two faces of debt, the good and the bad, in operation. And once again we see the gender dimension in a negative double whammy where women do not benefit as much as men from the student debt they acquire while also carrying the burden for longer.

How many students would have been able to afford a university education without the "golden passport" offered by student loans? Investing in ourselves by boosting our skills can ultimately raise our income, hopefully enabling us to more than repay them (although often this is not the case).

Student debt in the United Kingdom

Student debt[166] in the United Kingdom is more like a graduate tax than a loan. You only pay it back if you earn over a certain amount. As of 2022, if you earn under £25,000 a year[167] you will not be liable to repayments. However interest will still be charged at a rate which is somewhat contentious[168] so the balance of your loan will increase. Prior to 2022's new regulations, the government expected only around 25% of students to repay in full. That percentage will now go up as the government has increased the timeframe before loans are written off from 30 years to 40 years.

The average student debt in 2018 of students who finished their courses was £35,000[169] but there is a gender dimension.

The gender dimension of UK student debt

Female graduates carry the burden of student debt for fourteen years while their male counterparts carry it for only eleven years.[170] This might have something to do with the fact that female graduates starting salaries are £2,140 less than that of male graduates[171] (see Chapter Two for more information on this).

However, there is an extra dimension that kicks in for female graduates carrying student debt who go on to have children. A report shared by trade union Unison at the 2019 National Women's Conference[172] notes:

"The problem for our young women is that they often, because they have pregnancies, have breaks in their working lives to raise their children and so they incur greater interest on their student loans."

"The consequences for a young woman becoming a mother and taking maternity leave is that while she may not be repaying her student loan because her income drops below £25,000 per year while on maternity leave, interest still accrues on the outstanding loan. So she ends up having to pay back for more years and at greater cost than a comparable young man who does not take a year off work."

"So if a young woman leaves university at the same time as a comparable young man, they both commence employment in a similarly paid job, repaying their student loans at the same rate, they would complete their repayments at the same time. However, as soon as the young woman takes a maternity leave, she stops repayments because her earnings fall below the £25,000 threshold, she gets behind with her repayments, the duration of her loan grows and the outstanding debt continues to mount up due to the interest rates applied."

The Motherhood Penalty strikes again.

Student debt has become burdensome for many in the United Kingdom, but it is nothing compared to what many students in the United States face.

US student debt

US student debt is a different beast.

Senator Alexandria Ocasio-Cortez referenced the gargantuan difficulties graduates face in paying off their student loan debt. "It was literally easier for me to become the youngest woman in American history elected to Congress than it is to pay off my student loan debt," she declared at an event on Capitol Hill.[173]

In the US, young people and their dreams have been packaged into a highly profitable industry.

The Federal Reserve estimates in 2020 that Americans owed more than $1.7 trillion in student loans, an increase of 102% in the 10 years to 2020. Approximately 42 million Americans, roughly one in eight, have student loans. 6% of borrowers owe more than a hundred thousand dollars in student debts.

An earlier study by the Chamber of Commerce in 2016 showed that 60% of all US students had some form of debt by the time they graduated. One million had debts of over $100,000 and half a million students had debts of over $200,000. The average in 2016 was $37,102, a 78% increase from 2006. Average medical school debt in 2016 was $194,000.

The demographics of debt

77% of black students took out a federal loan to pay for higher education compared to 60% of all students. And the average debt on graduation in 2012 was $29,344 for black students compared to a national average of $25,640.

And this burden is worsened because Chamber of Commerce stats also show that among workers with a BA or higher qualification, black households as of 2016 earn 23% less than the median for the overall population making it harder for them to pay off their debt. And this shows up in the stats. 50% of black students who began college in 2003 defaulted due to financial insecurity within 12 years compared to 36% of Hispanic students and 21% of white students.

Women and student debt

This problem is particularly severe for women. While women account for 56% of undergraduates nationwide in the United States they hold almost 66% of total student debt[174] ($929 billion at the time) and the average debt on graduation is on average $31,276, 7% greater than that of men. This debt burden persists due to the gender pay gap which means that it takes longer for women to repay their debts.

This is particularly true for African American women. Persis Yu, director of the National Consumer Law Center's Student Loan Borrower Assistance Project notes that:

"African-American women with a graduate degree still earn less than white men with just a college degree. Because of the way that the labor market is set up, women, people of colour, and then especially women of colour, really need to get that credential in order to compete in the labor market. And so that means that they're going to take on a lot more debt."

The American Association of University Women estimates that, on average, white women with undergraduate student loan debt borrowed $31,346, while black women borrowed $37,558.[175]

The burden of student debt has been particularly onerous for millennials aged between 25 and 34 who have faced the recession which followed the Global Financial Crisis coupled with stagnant wages and rising tuition costs. For many of that generation, higher education has not then been the route to the promised land but has instead left them quagmired in debt.

Default

This means for many students that defaulting is the only option they can choose.

48% of borrowers who attend for-profit colleges default within 12 years, 12% of those who attend public colleges and 14% of those who attend non-profit colleges default.[176]

For those students, taking on debt does not deliver them to the promised land. Anything but.

So let's look at another golden passport aspect of debt - borrowing to start up or expand a business. Here we see an enormous gender chasm.

The "access to capital gap"

First, I want to emphasise the importance of this gap: its impact on wealth creation. Along with property ownership and the ownership of financial assets such as stock market investments, owning a business is one of the most powerful means of creating wealth. The returns on capital far exceed the returns on our labour. If it is more difficult for women to borrow money to set up businesses then it will be more difficult for us to create wealth in the greatest way that wealth is ever created.

Statistics show that women's share of the venture capital funding pie is so small as to be statistically insignificant.

A report published in 2019 by the British Business Bank showed less than 1% of total UK venture capital goes to female founded companies, while male founders get 89 per cent and mixed-gender teams get 10%.[177] 83% of deals that UK VCs made last year had no women at all on the founding teams. The report estimates that at the current rate of glacial progress, for all-female teams to reach even 10% of all deals will take until 2045).

Their 2022 report showed positive change, the authors citing: "Data from venture and capital growth firms ...showed... the proportion of deals concluded with all-female founder teams was 9%, up from 6% in 2020."[178]

The British Business Bank is owned by the government. It is its economic development bank whose self-avowed purpose is to make financial markets work better for small businesses - so it's in a perfect position to help tackle this underrepresentation.

When she was Chief Secretary to The Treasury, Liz Truss observed: "More women starting up businesses will supercharge economic growth. It's incredible that in 2019 men seem to have a virtual monopoly on venture capital. We need more investment going into start-up ventures and more women putting businesses forward. It's in everyone's interests that financing processes are open and meritocratic to grow the economy and make use of all the talent we have."

Truss also observed that women who start companies often believe it is vulgar to focus on making money and that we need to get over our squeamishness.

I don't think that's the whole story. Yes, we need to change our attitudes towards money, but... The whole patriarchal system that brings up girls and women to think money is a dirty word needs to change. That taboo needs to be comprehensively broken by both genders.

When it is, and when women's participation in venture capital funding grows, the results will benefit not just women but the entire economy.

In the meantime, our tiny share of VC finance begs the question, are these stats reflective of the ratio of women coming forward? It's hard to believe that less than 1% of promising VC opportunities are pitched by women. When you look at the small-business start up stats, you can see we are an entrepreneurial bunch.

The UK scores highly in international indexes of female entrepreneurship. 1 in 3 UK entrepreneurs is female, but, female-led businesses are, on average, only 44% of the size of male-led businesses, and male small businesses are five times more likely to scale up to £1million turnover than female equivalents[179].

Of course, to scale up requires capital.

So why are so few women entrepreneurs accessing this capital?

One answer might lie in the dominance of men and male-decision making in the VC field, with associated potential bias. Only 13% of senior people on UK investment teams are women, and almost half (48%) of investment teams have no women at all.[180]

Turning to the United States, we see a similar pattern of infinitesimally small participation by women in venture capital funding and decision making in a context of highly entrepreneurial women business founders.

According to a report by American Express,[181] woman-owned businesses are growing twice as fast on average as all businesses nationwide. The report notes: "In 2019, these U.S. women with diverse ethnic and geographic backgrounds started an average of 1,817 new businesses per day between 2018 and 2019, down only slightly from the record-setting 2018 number of 1,821."

Since the pandemic gathered pace in March of 2020, more women set up small businesses than men and were more likely to set up an entirely new venture on their own rather than buying into an existing company.[182] Again we see that women are highly entrepreneurial, but we're just not getting our hands on anything other than a tiny slice of the venture capital pie.

A report in the Harvard Business Review[183] by Ashley Bittner and Brigette Lau revealed that the percentage of VC deals that went to female-led startups declined in 2020 to 2.3%, down from 2.9% in 2019 which had been an all-time high!

Breaking into the boys' club?

The authors posit that it will probably take time for the reasons behind this drop to emerge but they speculate that the pandemic might have made investors more risk-averse and more likely to stick to their "existing networks — which is very much a "boys' club" and tougher for women to break into. And even when going outside their networks, many investors may be sticking with "pattern-matching habits, seeking the same kinds of companies that they've supported in the past, which are often tech companies led by men."

What we see again in the venture capital industry is what we have seen in the money world in general: the participation of women is extremely low.

About 12% of decision makers at VC firms in the US are women,[184] and, at the main decision-making partner levels, the presence of women is so small as to be statistically insignificant. Only 2.4% are female and most firms still don't have even a single female partner.

This is particularly pernicious as it is the founding partners who set the investment tone and carry the most power when deciding what ventures to back.

Just as the preponderance of male venture capitalists backing male-led startups creates a vicious cycle for women, the converse is also true. **When women venture capitalists do make the decisions, we're twice as likely to fund female teams.**

Startups founded by women employ two-and-a-half times more women than startups founded by men according to an analysis by Kauffman Fellows,[185] which also reveals that companies founded by women, with female executives, hire six times more women.

The financial returns on investing in women exceed those on investing in men

When women-led startups do get funded, they're more likely to be successful. They "ultimately deliver higher revenue — more than twice as much per dollar invested," a Boston Consulting Group analysis found.[186]

This report reveals that for every dollar of funding, female startups generated 78 cents, while male-founded startups generated just 31 cents.[187] Another study by a seed capital funding group, First Round Capital, substantiates these findings.[188] It notes that "companies with at least one female founder were meaningfully outperforming our investments in all-male teams." Out of the companies it funded, "those with a female founder performed 63% better than our investments with all-male founding teams."

Why is this? And why, given these findings do women seemingly still find it so difficult to obtain venture capital funding?

One theory put forward to explain the out-performance of female lead teams is that they and their ideas and business plans just have to be better and they have to work harder than male-lead teams in order to overcome the prejudices against them in the first place.

But the question remains: *why do those prejudices exist?*

We've seen above that it is not because women's projects do not perform well in terms of returns.

We saw above the suggestion that "existing networks, i.e. the "boys' club" means the venture capital world is tougher for women to break into either as decision-makers or as recipients of funding. "Pattern-matching habits," are also cited as a possible explanation, with funders seeking the same kinds of companies that they've supported in the past, which are overwhelmingly companies led by men. Another way to express this is in terms of "affinity bias" colloquially, same old same old...

I have to ask the question however: *are other conscious and unconscious biases at play? Biases on the part of men and women?*

Social Capital

Could women be self-limiting here? Believing there is no seat for us at the venture capitalist's table or are we knocking on the door and being turned away? We come here again to the idea of social capital, to the idea that certain realms are either open to us and within our grasp or just too far out of reach. It's a vicious cycle at the moment - if there were more women involved in venture capital funding, more female-led starts ups would be funded. This increase in the female presence on both sides of this equation would in turn help to break down the 'pattern matching habits' and 'affinity' biases which are part of what is currently holding us back.

To sum up

As well as a gender dimension to debt there is also a racial dimension with women of colour being particularly adversely served by debt.

We've been on the wrong side of the debt equation consistently throughout history, less able to access mortgages than men because of income gaps and confidence gaps but also because some of the mortgage products on offer have been mis-sold to women, particularly to women of colour, costing them more and exposing them to a higher level of risk than would be the case if they were a man with identical financial circumstances.

But, thanks to machine-based algorithmic lending platforms, gender and racial discrimination in areas like mortgage lending, particularly in the United States is decreasing.

Pay gaps and the confidence gap also explains why in the United Kingdom, fewer women can get on the property ladder than men.

Despite the existence of the pay gap in the United States, seemingly psychological and structural reasons have inverted this with more single women buying property than single men.

In the UK, because of the gender pay gap and the gender confidence/aspirations gap, when we take on student loans, we carry that debt for longer.

In the US women carry around two thirds of student debt and borrow more than men to fund their university education. Black women borrow more than white women. The cost of US student debt means that a high percentage of students default.

One of the most powerful wealth creators that exists is venture capital funding but women's share of this in the UK and the US is negligible and yet when we do get funded the return on funding women is considerably greater than that of funding men. You get far more bang for your buck investing in women so why don't more people invest in women? Probably a legacy of prejudice, unconscious bias and possibly also women feeling that we don't belong at the venture capital table which is not surprising when it is inhospitable to us. This reinforces the point that it is crucial to get more women into decision-making positions as lenders whether it be mortgage lenders or venture capital lenders so that we can make the money world more appealing and accessible to women.

If we do that, we all benefit.

What governments can do:

- Wield the sex discrimination acts to penalise and reform companies practising discriminatory practices
- Recognise that the access to capital gap inhibits economic growth
- Spread that word and create initiatives to diminish that gap

What companies can do:

- The money world needs to make itself more hospitable to us so that we can engage more with it
- Become aware of and break down biases such as affinity bias and pattern-matching habits that shut unfamiliar borrowers – in this case women – out of the venture capital magic circle
- Know that lack of diversity on your board and in the companies

you invest in, is costing you
- Become more diverse - a female presence in decision-making roles mean more female-led opportunities are funded
- Increase your return on investment - know that the returns on investing in female-led start-ups exceed those of male-founded ventures - diversify your investment practices

What you can do if you are a woman seeking funding:

- Apply to venture capitalists with at least one, preferably more, women in decision making positions
- If Liz Truss is correct and you are squeamish about talking money or profits, lose that squeamishness
- Ask for you what you need. Women tend to lowball it
- Focus on the figures. It's harder to argue with numbers than concepts
- Network with the female financial community to increase your social capital

What we all can do:

- Become more financially literate
- When we are, *believe* that we are
- Rid ourselves of any remaining financial squeamishness and educate our daughters accordingly
- Be on guard - women and minorities have historically been charged more for debt than their particular circumstances warrant and have had more toxic forms of debt pushed upon them
- Recognise predatory lenders and predatory loans for the toxic traps they are and recognise how manipulative those providers can be and have been
- Know that even though they are decreasing, gender and racial prejudice in the mortgage sector remain.
- Befriend fintech to help get on the property ladder and to access cheaper mortgages - algorithmic machine-based mortgage lending is a major friend to women, and people of colour and minorities

- Be aware that the new changes in the law in the UK will increase the burden of student debt on students and that inflation will further increase the burden and cost
- Help yourself to pay off your student debt sooner – aim higher (see the section on the pay gap and aspiration/conditioning gap for more information here)

Chapter Seven: The ugly side of debt

Debt in disguise

Buy Now Pay Later, aka, Buy Now Pain Later, consuming more than you otherwise would

- Use of BNPL quadrupled in 2020 in the UK

- 75% of users are female

- BNPL is effectively debt in disguise with all of the costs and few of the benefits

- It is predicated on severing a psychological brake to our spending and manipulating us into spending more

- Its business model is predicated in large part, on making us spend more than we otherwise would

- Klarna in its advertising to vendors suggests that people using its services will spend *33% more than normal*

- 2022 gross merchandise volume of Klarna alone rose 42% to $80 billion

- BNPL is inexplicably linked to to fast fashion (with all the problems that creates which we shall examine later)

- 56% of millennials said BNPL encouraged them to spend money they could not afford, with 36% of them experiencing resulting financial difficulties which damaged their relationships and health

- 1 in 10 customers of BNPL schemes have been contacted by debt collection companies after falling behind on payments

- 45% of users had missed at least one payment over the previous 12 months with 48% of users incurring additional fees and 56% of them being unable to pay back other debt such as overdrafts, loans or credit cards as a result

Instant gratification

Buy Now Pay Later sounds wonderful doesn't it? Like a bridge to a happier place. 10 million people – 20% of UK adults - used BNPL during lockdown.[189] Its use quadrupled in 2020.[190]

What a friendly facilitator it sounds. If you haven't got sufficient funds in your bank account, let that not hold you back. You do not have to wait for that coveted dress, jacket, shoes. You do not have to delay gratification. It can be yours now! The retailer will fund your purchase. It will borrow on your behalf. When you arrive at the checkout, online or physical, you get offered the option of paying later, in one, two or sometimes three instalments delayed over several months.

And yes I get that that can be fun (and sometimes incredibly helpful), but like most kinds of fun it has a dark side. And, if you're not very careful, what starts off serving you flips around until you are the servant. It is marketed as a seamless, friction-free way of purchasing what you want, but this very lack of friction can lead you down a very slippery slope.

The dark side

Let's start with how BNPL presents itself.

Debt in disguise

If you are already maxed out on credit cards you might console yourself with the thought that BNPL is not debt. After all, it is the retailer that is financing the borrowing, not you, the consumer.

But, make no mistake, BNPL is consumer debt by any other name. And more than that, it's supercharged debt, the crack cocaine of debt, far more dangerous, potent and addictive than other forms.

I'll show you how.

   1) **Lack of protection**

The BNPL companies are taking on the credit card companies at their own game, and winning. This is not good news for you because unlike the credit card companies, BNPL does not offer you the same protection.

At the moment some of the BNPL lenders (Klarna and Clearpay) are regulated by the Financial Conduct Authority but protections offered are nowhere near as extensive as they would be under the 1974 Consumer Credit Act. If BNPL were considered credit, it would be covered. But it is not. Because of a clever technical wheeze.

These schemes are *not* considered credit because "loans" are paid back in under a year and do not charge interest. Instead "late payment fees" are charged. Essentially interest by another name.

The Consumer Credit Act[191] protects consumers and makes lenders give warnings about the risks of taking on debt before signing up to it. Because BNPL schemes are not regulated in the same way that companies offering conventional credit are, they don't come with the same warnings that might make consumers think twice before taking on the debt.

Lending covered by the Consumer Credit Act also requires a cooling off period and forces lenders to check that borrowers can afford to meet repayment schedules as well as providing cover for credit card purchases of between £100 and £30,000 if goods purchased are faulty or do not arrive.

But BNPL is not covered. There is no ombudsman to protect people pursuing these schemes when things go wrong.

Also, because many of the BNPL merchants like Klarna perform a "soft" rather than "hard" credit check they do not screen out customers with debt problems in the same way that a hard credit check would. i.e. they do not protect you from yourself in the same way.

2) Overspending - materialistic opium

The business model of BNPL is predicated on making you spend more than normal. Klarna in its advertising to vendors suggest that people using its services will spend *33% more than normal.* Klarna is compensated by vendors for this additional spending. Retailers give it and other BNPL merchants a percentage of every spend.

64% of the Gen Zers who used BNPL during lockdown said that paying with BNPL made them spend more than normal,[192] becoming, a kind of materialistic opium.

Research conducted by Hastee's annual workplace wellbeing study[193] reported that 56% of millennial workers said such schemes encouraged them to spend money they could not afford. Millennials were hardest hit saying 36% experienced difficulties with this impacting their relationships and health.

3) **This urge to overspend, coupled with the disguised nature of BNPL veils and worsens the potential consequences - BNPL and debt collection agencies**

Things can go wrong very quickly, starting with when you miss your payments. Then you get charged "late payment fees" and you run the risk of your debt being passed on to a debt collection agency. The Citizens Advice charity reported in September 2021 that 1 in 10 customers of BNPL schemes have been contacted by debt collection companies after falling behind on payments. 96% of people contacted said it caused them sleepless nights and made their mental health worse. Millie Harris, a debt advisor at Citizens Advice East Devon,[194] said: "my concern is that people aren't processing the fact that buy now pay later is credit. They don't realise there are going to be consequences if they don't pay – it gives them a false sense of security."

The increase in young people going bankrupt

Accounting firm RSM notes that between 2016 and 2019 there was a tenfold increase in young people going bankrupt. Those consumers who failed to pay off their debts saw them passed onto a debt collection agency.

Clearly not all of this can be explained by use of BNPL but I'm willing to hazard a guess that it has played a role.

4) **Default and damage to credit scores**

Research firm CompareThemarket.com suggests that 41% of consumers were unaware that missing a payment, a.k.a. "partial default" would give them a black mark on their credit scores, potentially impacting their ability to access debt or mortgages longer term, and the potential costs of such debt - a case of buy now and *really* pay for it later.

This is concerning because the same research shows that pre-lockdown 45% of users had missed at least one payment over the previous 12 months with 48% of users incurring additional fees and 56% of them stating that late payment has resulted in them being unable to pay back other debt such as overdrafts, loans or credit cards.

5) **Exploitative marketing of the most vulnerable - buy now pay later and age**

Data indicates 25% of users are aged 18-24 and 50% are aged 25-36.[195]

23% of 18 to 24-year-olds said they are likely to use such schemes to keep them going.[196]

16% of Gen Zers used BNPL since lockdown. That compares with the general adult population where only 7% have made a BNPL purchase.

That's not surprising because the same research suggests that it is younger purchasers who were being targeted: 33% of generation Z said that they'd noticed more BNPL plans being offered to them since lockdown compared to 18% of general UK shoppers who had noticed more such promotions.

This is particularly concerning because young people have been more than disproportionately hit by the Covid lockdown seeing them furloughed or lose their jobs altogether which will imperil their ability to repay this debt. 1 in 8 young people under 34 years of age have been chased by debt collection companies due to late payments, a higher percentage than older age cohorts. Charity Payplan[197] said that 73% of its clients from 18 to 34 claimed that BNPL deals created debt problems for them.

The gender dimension of BNPL

Young women shopping for clothes and footwear are fuelling the boom in BNPL according to a government review.[198]

This review reports that 75% of users are female and 90% of transactions involve fashion and footwear.

What this means is when BNPL becomes a problem, it is disproportionately a problem for women.

Why do BNPL schemes make you more likely to overspend? Psychological manipulation

I note above that Klarna itself in its advertising to vendors suggests from its own data that people using its services will spend *33% more than normal.*[199] BNPL schemes are predicated on severing the psychological brake that acts on purchasing.

There's a dopamine hit when we buy things but if we have to hand over cold, hard cash *physically* when we buy, that pleasure is matched by the pain of reducing the money in our wallet.

Distancing ourselves by using debit cards is one step towards severing this psychological brake but with a debit card we still see the money coming out of our account electronically so there is an element of pain to curtail us.

With BNPL there is no pain for 30 days or more *but there is pleasure today.*

Our rational brains might know this is not good for us but as is so often the case, logic is trumped by emotion.

The Cash Illusion

I wrote extensively in my last book, *10 Things Everyone Needs to Know About Money*, about what economists call the cash illusion, about the fact that what we used to pay influences how much we spend. If we use credit cards we are more likely to spend more than if we used cash.

I would suggest that using BNPL will exacerbate that tendency because of the way it has been packaged and because it is not subject to the same restraints and controls and oversight that we have seen on credit cards, thereby allowing more vulnerable individuals access to its products.

BNPL instead of being a facilitator can negatively impact our financial resilience.

By assuming that all will be well and that we'll be able to make our payments 1, 2 and 3 months down the line, we're introducing a degree of vulnerability to our financial life that is not helpful. One of the goals of this book is to help increase our financial resilience. BNPL is a direct threat to that.

The fightback against BNPL

Stella Creasy, the Labour MP for Walthamstow, previously ran an excellent campaign reigning in some of the more stomach-churning excesses of the payday loan industry. Creasy notes: "if you're feeling low working from home there is a real issue facilitated by these BNPL schemes which rely on the emotional connection people make with someone whose life they want to live, rather than the boring details of can they afford it."

Alice Tapper has founded a financial website called *Go Fund Yourself* and has created a campaign called *#KlarNaa*. Tapper was inspired by the experience of Hannah Kelly, a 23 year old student who bought clothes and handbags using Laybuy, Klarna and Very, but was unable to pay off the debts before they started incurring interest. Over four years, her debts snowballed to £12,500.

Martin Lewis from Money Saving Expert[200] said, "these firms target shoppers to use credit to spend on things they wouldn't otherwise buy, which is dangerous. It is absolutely luring people into debt and it will lead to problems unless properly controlled." He has called on the Financial Conduct Authority to intervene. The Advertising Standards Authority already has intervened, publishing guidelines which banned retailers from saying that such deals were risk free and instructing them to be clearer about the nature of their product. The government is currently mulling this over.[201]

But we are not powerless here.

Let's switch off the manipulation. Here's a psychological hack that will help our financial and mental health.

Pay now consume later

Research has shown that if we switched from a *buy now pay later* mindset to a *pay now consume later* mindset we could increase our happiness as thinking about future events has been shown to trigger stronger emotions than thinking about the same events in the past. I think most of us know that part of the joy of a holiday is the anticipation itself. This is borne out by further research by the same authors which shows that money spent on experiences such as travel, concerts and sporting events rather than on material goods gives us more happiness.[202]

Debt is linked to consumerism, taken out to buy stuff we really don't need, but there is also a large swath of borrowers who borrow out of desperation just to make ends meet, as we saw in the previous chapters.

To sum up:

Buy Now Pay Later schemes have been growing in popularity dramatically in recent years. While they can be a helpful facilitator of our purchases, too often they make us overspend, leading to financial problems down the road. BNPL companies are the Peter Pan of spending, luring us into a kind of never-never land where there are no consequences. Until there are. Until the bailiffs call.

When we delve deeper, the dark side of BNPL becomes evident. Yes it facilitates, but it also distorts consumer behaviour. This kind of **stealth credit** is a dangerous drug. The premise of painless purchasing is highly manipulative.

It is predicated on severing a necessary psychological brake which limits our spending and ironically, rather than increasing our happiness tends to do the opposite. If we flip the equation and we pay now and consume later, we would actually increase our happiness.

Do we really want to allow ourselves to be manipulated in this way?

Debt is a powerful drug. All too easily we can become addicted, as with drugs, to get our fix will need ever higher levels of debt. Owing to the power of compound interest debt multiplies faster than our ability to repay it. To pay off our debts, we need to take on other debts as everyone who has a revolving stack of credit cards, or has had the dubious services of a payday loan lender, will know all too well.

And my analogy continues. As with drugs, there are pushers of debt, the credit card companies that send us unsolicited applications, the Buy Now Pay Later merchants who knowingly exploit the psychological interplay that makes us buy *more* when we pay *later*; the predatory lenders responsible for the explosion of the sub-prime mortgage market in the United States.

Addictus - debt and enslavement

Even the word "addict" originates with the debt slaves of ancient Rome. Someone who is unable to discharge his or her debts to another person became their debt slave, became their "addictus." That is where the word "addict" comes from - being enslaved.

I give you debt, my friends.

What government needs to do:

- Close the loophole that allows BNPL companies to not be subject to the same controls, protections and oversight as traditional lenders

What companies need to do:

- BNPL companies need to be much more transparent about the downsides of using their services such as: overspending, lack of consumer protection and adverse credit consequences down the road
- The entire loan industry needs to be able to discover levels of BNPL indebtedness in consumers so it can make lending decisions

more in alignment with those consumers' financial integrity - i.e. not create 'problem debt' scenarios by loaning to people already under debt distress

What we can do:

- Recognise BNPL for what it is – debt in disguise
- Be aware of the levels of manipulation that are being deployed against you by BNPL companies
- Know that using BNPL makes it more likely you will overspend
- Know that the BNPL does not offer the same productions as other debt products such as credit cards
- Recognise that missing a payment can give you a black mark on your credit score, negatively impacting your ability to borrow in the future
- Beware of a general trend which is seeing increasing levels of bankruptcy amongst young people
- Be aware that as a woman you are particularly exposed to BNPL via fast fashion (more on that later)
- Understand the nature of the cash illusion – the more we use credit, the more likely we are to spend more than if we stuck to cash
- Befriend cash - it helps reduce your spending and gives you freedom (this is particularly important in cases of domestic abuse)
- Explore the happiness dividend of a *pay now consume later* practice such as paying in advance for holidays

Chapter Eight: Women and spending

How to spend better

- Ubiquitous external manipulations affect our spending

- The global marketing machine is expert at creating needs we never knew we had

- These false needs provide fleeting pleasure but impose huge costs on our financial and mental health, and on the health of our planet

- The fashion and beauty industries spend billions of dollars every year telling women how we should look, and how we shouldn't, which undermines our sense of self and makes us spend billions more in pursuit of unrealistic, unsustainable and unhealthy stereotypes

- Our consumerist society veils and promotes emotional spending which can easily turn into addiction.

- A scarcity complex is hardwired into our brains, born of the anomaly of affluence. This creates in us an unquenchable desire to consume

- As a species, our spending and consuming is out of control

- Global clothing production doubled between 2000 and 2014

- In 2019, in the UK, we spent £61 billion on new clothes

- We hoard £47 billion worth of it, 3.6 billion items of clothing we just don't wear, 57 items each on average

- We discard 13 million items of clothing *every week,* most of which ends up in landfill

- We need to understand the high price of cheap clothes. the fashion industry:

- Consumes 93,000,000,000 m³ of water – enough to supply 5 million people

- Is responsible for more carbon emissions and all international flights and maritime shipping combined.

- Is heavily correlated with economic slavery and the abuse of women

The above chapters show the burden of debt we carry and the damage that debt can do. The irony is much of the consumer debt we take on is to buy things we don't really need, which give us just fleeting pleasures, that clutter our homes and clog up landfill when we dispose of them.

Even if we don't finance these purchases by debt, we could seriously improve our financial health by not buying them at all.

One of the most powerful ways to improve our financial freedom, health and future is to *spend less*. Simple and obvious, yes. Powerful, yes. Easy? No.

A whole array of forces are lined up to extract our hard-earned money from us. They are so powerful and insidious that we don't even know they're doing it much of the time.

The cost of glamour

The pressures on women to look a certain way, to sport the "right" clothes or body shape or hair and make up… All this costs us in time and money (and let's face it, time is also money). Back in 1990, Naomi Wolf's book *The Beauty Myth* exposed how corporates exploited women's aesthetic insecurities, offering us costly solutions to problems or insufficiencies we never knew we had. And so it goes on. Cellulite, cankles, thin eyebrows, thick eyebrows, curly hair, straight hair, absence of contours, too many contours, failed pencil test, failed thigh gap…

And it's only got worse thanks to the amplification of social media, and fashion magazines pushing the perfect image, and retailers continuing to push the perfect products, conveniently side-stepping the issue of whether or not we have enough money to buy them. Buy Now Pay Later, the Neverland of money, solves that as we saw above. But there's always a crocodile and it comes in the form of the ticking clock of pay later and if you don't pay later then the bailiffs come knocking. Not quite so glamorous.

To all of this I would say: ***nothing looks as good as freedom feels.***

Negative and positive freedoms

We've seen countless examples where the money world does not serve women well. Our *negative freedoms* as they are called - the freedoms we have externally to act without hindrances such as prejudice, lack of safety, closed doors, glass ceilings, legal constraints or prohibitions - have improved over the centuries, but there's still a long way to go.

Now it's time to take a look at our *positive freedoms* - the freedoms we give ourselves, where we are liberated from internal constraints. Time to examine how these can and do damage our financial health.

There are two main forms these take

- Self limiting beliefs - "I'm no good with money," or "investing in the stock market is incomprehensible to me," or "I really don't understand the whole pension thing," none of which is surprising given how the money world speaks to women.[203] But the reality of these beliefs is that we are effectively closing doors on ourselves
- Multiple external manipulations that infiltrate our subconscious. These are particularly insidious - if we're not aware of them, how can we fight them? These are the traps, so well disguised we don't know we've stepped into them and we can't see the exit

How do we fight these? We fight the self-limiting beliefs by analysing and understanding where they come from so that we might challenge and adjust them. And by continuing to try to change how the money world speaks to, treats and welcomes us.

We fight the external manipulations by dragging these invisible enemies out of the shadows.

External manipulation - the consumption trap - the creation of needs we never knew we had

The marketing and advertising industries, bolstered by social media platforms like Instagram and Facebook, create in us needs we never knew we had, needs that do not serve us, the satisfaction of which provides only temporary utility and which come at considerable cost to our financial health, and ultimately also to the health of our planet itself.

These needs, however, do serve the companies that run the consumption sector. There is a direct conflict of interest here. This is huge business and as with the debt industry, while we might think we are the consumers, we are in many ways the consumed.

Any time you see *must have,* shut your wallet/laptop and run a mile.

The extent of commercial exploitation here is alarming.

To better understand our own behaviour in the face of this, it's time to dig down deeper into the realm of psychology.

Why do we spend?

Most of our spending is what we would call *nondiscretionary spending* – mortgage or rent, food, travel, health spending, essential support of family members, insurance, car and home maintenance, essential clothes such as school uniform or work clothes.

Beyond that, and for those of us who are lucky enough to have some money left over, we get into discretionary spending - holidays, entertainment, music, restaurants, non-essential clothes, luxuries, however we define those.

Before we can examine what healthy spending looks like, let's start with unhealthy spending as there are many lessons we can learn from it. *How not to* can be flipped on its head into *how to.*

Unhealthy spending - emotional spending

Often we will buy things to make ourselves feel better, in response to an emotional upset, to stress, to keep up - essentially from feelings of inadequacy that somehow we are not enough but that buying this whatever it is will make us *feel* enough.

The satisfaction here is temporary and the spending of money does not deal with the root cause of the desire to spend it.

When we spend emotionally the limbic old brain is taking control and making us spend impulsively. It's not predicated on logic but on our emotions. Talking ourselves out of it with logic will not work unless we unearth and fully understand the emotions with which we are dealing so that we can acknowledge and address them in a healthy way.

Psychological hack

We do that by taking the time to ask ourselves questions - *will this make me feel happy in a year's time or will this push me into debt and harm my financial goals, **or will saving the money make me feel even better?** Or why am I even doing this? What do I hope to feel or gain? What feelings might I be trying to escape from?*

Physical hack

We also need to break the moment by maybe going into a different room, ringing a friend, doing some yoga or meditation, or hoovering and putting on a load of laundry. If you're shopping, online or physically, get outside for some fresh air, have a coffee, sit on a bench and people watch. Break that moment and interrupt the impulse.

This will help create a distance that removes the impulsivity and can help us apply logic and clarity. In psychological terms, we overrule the limbic system by activating the prefrontal cortex.

Reframe what something costs

Another way to analyse our spending and deploy both logic and emotion to serve us is to calculate how much we earn per hour so that next time we contemplate buying a £200 pair of shoes and we realise we have to work 2.5 full days to get them (you need to look at your post-tax income to make the calculation) you might think twice, you might think conceptually and emotionally you'd rather have 2.5 days off.

And here's an extra incentive and financial planning hack to help us: the average stock market return in the UK over a ten year period is 9.2%.[204] So if you left those shoes on the shelf and invested in a tracker fund instead for 15 years, reducing the compounding rate to 5% to take account of fees and to be a bit more conservative, the future value of those unbought shoes would be £416 pounds. That's a permanent benefit in the way that an extra pair of shoes can never be.

Because the global marketing machine encourages us to buy at every turn from the *"because you're worth it"* mantra, to the *"must have"* shout, to the *'it's payday, reward yourself!'* siren call, it can be hard to see when our spending becomes unhealthy. When emotional spending tips into addiction.

Personal note

I'm going to share Ann's story[205] below:

"Unintentionally for me, my bits of spending to cheer myself up became a habit. Each time I felt down, I would go shopping to cheer myself up. A habit is created by repeating an action often enough for it to become the norm, a bit like smoking, starting on one or two cigarettes a day, and then ending up getting addicted and smoking a box of 20. Well, shopping grabbed me in the same way.

I wish there would have been a health warning like there are on wine bottles and cigarettes, because when we spend as a way to bridge our personal or professional pressures, that's when the danger lies because our low moods are transformed to highs, and we only have to do that a number of times before a habit can pave its way forward and even lead to an addiction. I now help other people realise that spending as a way to bridge mental health pressure, is addictive. It really doesn't make you feel better, but it creates even more of a problem than you already had because not only have you got your unaddressed problems to face, you also now have a habit or even an addiction to kick, as well as maybe debts that have escalated out of control."

Oniomania

Oniomania is literally, a mania for making purchases, and this is what ensnared Ann.

The thing about addiction is that whatever our substance or pastime of choice is, it never heals or cures us. It simply distracts us temporarily from our pain, from the underlying wound which is going to fester and continue festering. The substance or activity enables us to keep avoiding the problem, but the price we pay for avoidance can be incalculably high.

I'm only too aware that overcoming addictions can feel like an impossible mountain to climb yet so many of us do climb those mountains and emerge on the other side. There are various resources at the end of the book that can help with various spending addictions.

Substance addiction is beyond the scope of this book but one of the best books I have read on it is called *In The Realm of the Hungry Ghosts* by Gabor Mate. Another wonderful book that helps us learn to heal our wounds and understand ourselves better is Dr Nicole la Pena's *How to Do The Work.*

When we are able to overcome this tendency /compulsion /addiction by dealing with the underlying problem, and consequently remove the power and the control that emotional spending has over us, we feel better twice over. We have improved our mental health and improved our positive freedom to act by helping us withstand the seductions of the consumption trap.

And we will be amassing a nice pot of savings that will help our future abundance.

We need to reign in our consumerism and not just for our own sakes.

As a species, our spending and consuming is out of control.

We are over consuming things that give us just a momentary joy.

We have become hooked on fast fashion, acquisition, shopping as a spiritual God without soul, without spirit.

The high price of cheap clothes

I'm not suggesting we stop consuming. I'm suggesting we stop over-consuming. That we consume mindfully. I'm suggesting we take a long hard look at the fashion industry and end our love affair with fast fashion.

The environmental cost of production and distribution

According to UNCTAD,[206] the fashion industry consumes 93 billion cubic metres of water - enough to supply five million people - and spits out half a million tons of microfibre into the ocean every year.

A World Bank report[207] notes: "The fashion industry is responsible for 10% of annual global carbon emissions, more than all international flights and maritime shipping combined. At this pace, the fashion industry's greenhouse gas emissions will surge more than 50 % by 2030."

The dominant business model in the sector is "fast fashion", a dizzying conveyor belt of constantly changing collections of cheap clothes, with buyers encouraged to buy and discard clothes as if they were disposable. The doubling in global clothing production between 2000 and 2014 bears testament to this overproduction.[208]

Fast fashion is also susceptible to high levels of returns. Research from KPMG reveals that returns cost British retailers £7 billion a year and that many goods go to landfill because they can't be sold on.

Let's look at the life story of some of these clothes.

The social costs are paid by the many and the abnormal profits reaped by the few

The life story of fast fashion clothes encompasses a journey that takes in extreme poverty at one end and extreme wealth at the other. The fabric is likely to have been produced in Eastern Africa then exported to Bangladesh or India, where women toil in sweatshops on subsistence wages to transform fabric into garments, which are exported again at rock bottom prices, shipped or flown around the world then sold with sufficient markup to bolster the fortunes of the billionaire clothing kings who control this trade, and the legions of the wannabe billionaires keen to follow in their footsteps.

Economic enslavement

The Global Slavery Index's 2018 report[209] estimates that $127.7 billion worth of garments are produced by people vulnerable to economic enslavement, as part of a global economy that trapped 40.3 million people in modern slavery, 71% of whom were women.

The economic, social and environmental cost of excess consumption

According to a survey by M&S and Oxfam published in 2016, consumers in the UK in 2019 spent a record £61 billion on new clothes. That's more than any other country in Europe and double what the Italians spend.

And we don't even use much of it. We hoard £46.7 billion of it. That money bought us 3.6 billion items of clothing we just don't wear.[210] That averages out at 57 items each, with 16 items worn just once, and the price tags still dangling on 11. Apparently one in 20 people have over 50 items still with the tags on.

Wardrobe rage

This stuff does not spark joy. In fact, the opposite is true. The same survey reports that 49% of us suffer 'wardrobe rage.' We have too much stuff. We can't find what we want, and/or we can't make up our mind what to wear. Our wardrobes and often our partners feel the rage.

The environmental cost of disposal

In an attempt to regain control, we discard an estimated 13 million items of clothing every week.[211] Some goes to landfill, some is resold domestically and almost 400,000 tonnes are exported to buyers every year.[212]

Much of this ends up in Ghana. Around 15 million items of clothing arrive weekly, mainly from the UK.[213] Around 40% of this, an estimated 50 tonnes a day, is discarded, ending up in landfill, becoming mountains of clothes which overflow onto beaches. The fibres rot, and release a toxic stew that contaminates land and sea.

Funeral pyres of clothes

"We've completely devalued what clothing is" says environmentalist Liz Rickets.[214] "I don't know how we come back from treating fashion like a plastic bag or a plastic bottle." Ricketts was in Accra in Ghana in August 2019 when the methane generated in one of the clothing dumps exploded. As of 2020, it was still burning.

Our obsession with fast fashion is polluting Ghanaian air, land and sea. Not to mention the environmental cost of getting it there in the first place.

Dead white men's clothes

It wasn't always like this. Once upon a time, in the decade following the 1960s when these markets first flourished, the second hand clothes were high quality, durable and reusable. The perception was that the only way an owner would have parted company with them was at death. In honour of this they were called *obroni wawu* - dead white man's clothes.

Now the owner who disposes of their clothes is very much alive.

Do we really need all this stuff?

The question is why do we buy it? I think the answer lies in the brilliant introduction to *The Affluent Society* by the late economist John Kenneth Galbraith.

Galbraith said: "Nearly all people, in nearly all nations, for nearly all of human history, have been poor. Widespread poverty is not an anomaly. Widespread affluence is."

So a scarcity complex is hardwired into our brains, into the old lizard brains that really control so much of what we do. Not our sophisticated, aware brain but the primal urge brain.

So does our scarcity complex make us hardwired to consume?

I think it does. We haven't yet learned to navigate our relationship with stuff.

But stuff hasn't made us happy. We end up working longer hours to service the debts we incur in amassing stuff. We believe stuff is the solution to our problems, to our low moods and we attempt to buy our way out of trouble. All this is just displacement activity. All we are doing is distancing ourselves from dealing with the real problem, which is why we are feeling low in the first place.

Fleeting pleasures can beat grand gestures

A study called *if money doesn't make you happy then you probably aren't spending it right* [215] suggests spending small amounts of money on a series of small fleeting pleasures that enhance daily life rather than saving up to blow it on a big purchase, the novelty of which inevitably wears off. This is known as the "endowment effect."

Why even the super-rich get bored by their yachts and are in a perpetual quest to get bigger ones.

They, we, all of us, get used to stuff and we need another hit. Even for the super-rich, enough is never enough. The novelty of something, no matter how wonderful it might have seemed, always wears off.

Healthy spending. The dividends of non consumption

Think what we could do with all the money we could save not buying these clothes. Think of all the extra leisure time we could enjoy not having to work the hours to buy those clothes, or to pay off the debts we amass in buying them. Think of the environmental dividends we could create by not buying those clothes.

If we can save, if we can conserve our own precious resources and invest them for our own future, we can also do that for our planet, for our environment.

To sum up:

Huge external manipulations affect our spending, making us attempt to conform to externally created ideas of how women should look, or buying things we never knew we wanted.

As a species, our consuming and spending are out of control. Are unsustainable.

The consumerist, disposable society in which we live masks a multitude of problems from emotional spending, to spending addiction, to industrial production processes that degrade our planet and enslave female employees and then degrade the planet even further when we dispose of the billions of items of clothing we never really wanted in the first place.

Not only are we being manipulated into wanting these things, we are seduced into buying them by the availability and proliferation of 'easy money' - particularly BNPL shemes which serve the companies involved but ultimately serve us far less and very often damage us.

What governments can do:

- Promote a circular economy where we recycle and reuse items in a more sustainable way
- Promote initiatives to reveal the true costs of producing an item, which involves the extraction of resources to produce it, the energy used to produce it and transport it and in turn move it to a disposal site, and the environmental cost of its dumping and decay

What companies can do:

- Analyse and publicise the true costs of production (this could work in the same way that food companies now have to list ingredients and warn of allergens. There's no reason why garments and household items couldn't come with a health warning)
- Many companies already do attempt to have carbon neutral

production methods but equally important are carbon neutral distribution methods

What we can do:

- Beware the consumption trap
- Understand the scarcity complex hardwired into our brains, which programmes us to consume, and over-consume,
- Any time you see *must have,* shut your wallet/laptop and run a mile
- Root out the causes of emotional spending and understand how it can easily tip into addiction
- Deploy the psychological hack of asking questions:
- Do we really need all this stuff?
- Will this make me feel happy in a year's time?
- Will this push me into debt and harm my financial goals
- Will saving the money make me feel even better?
- Why am I even doing this?
- What do I hope to feel?
- What feelings might I be trying to escape from?
- Pause
- Deploy the physical hack of breaking the moment to do something else - a healthy displacement activity
- Understand the cost to ourselves and the economic, social and environmental costs of excess consumption particularly with regard to fashion
- Beware fast fashion
- Reframe what something costs in terms of the time you have to work to afford it
- In terms of the true costs of its production to our financial and overall health and that of the planet
- Seek sustainability in our own finances
- Pursue sustainable consumption practices
- Support those companies that produce sustainably and shun those that don't
- Switch to healthy spending and reap the dividends of non-consumption and saving
- Remember, nothing looks as good as freedom feels

Chapter Nine: Women and saving

How to save more

- **In the UK**, there is an 32% gender savings gap

- Female millennials have a 60% savings gap - equivalent to £15,900

- Gen Z women have a 47% gender savings gap

- But, women are slightly more inclined than men to practice saving - 73% of women compared with 71% of men

- In couples, 46% of women and 45% of men are saving.

- Having children changes this

- One year after the birth of a child, 42% of men are still managing to save while only 34% of women are doing so

- Ten years after the birth, 46% of men are saving compared with 40% of women

- **In the US**, men are more likely than women (42% vs. 24%) to put extra money into savings, while women are more likely than men (42% vs. 29%) to use extra money to pay off bills or debt

- Over 50% of women have zero savings compared to 39% of men

- 23% of women have less than $1,000 saved compared to 25% of men

- In every other category up to $50,000 and above, men are saving more

- Being "future orientated" helps us save but only if we possess financial knowhow

Those who cannot save

First of all, I have to issue the caveat that I fully understand that for many women, saving *anything* is just not an option. Their reality is that they cannot make ends meet from one end of the month to the next. I know that as a result of the cost of living crunch the number of people in financial crisis will increase.

My heart goes out to them all and I hope and pray that the state can and does step in to support them and that charities too can play their part, and that their financial health can change for the better.

There is a big community of wonderful women out there helping other women in that position. Please see further resources at the end of the book.

Those who can save

This book is aimed at those women who *do* have disposable income, would like to have more and to make better use of it.

We've seen above the dividends of non-consumption and how psychology is deployed against us to extract money from us. Well, we can deploy psychology equally well to hold onto it. In this chapter I will show you how to marry the psychological insights with practical, *how to* knowledge so that we can save more while enjoying the journey as well as the destination.

So that's start with a look at the gendered angle and then we will move on to the *how to.*

Gender differences in saving

Data from various studies come up with different totals depending on samples and methodology but consistently show that in both the United Kingdom and the United States, men are saving more than women. This is not surprising given gender pay gaps - it's another manifestation of the consequences of these gaps. It can also be used as a comparative measure of our financial resilience, or of our financial precarity.

A study in the UK by VoucherCodes[216] shows nearly one in five (18%) of all UK adults has zero savings.

Those who do have savings, have an average of £20,993.01. The average man has £27,638.12, the average woman £15,312.59 - a gender savings gap of 45%.

The same survey examined annual savings patterns. The average person saves £2,007.18 per year: men saving £2,440.52 on average compared to women's £1,629.18. A gap of 33%.

The biggest gender disparities in saving are seen in the aged 35-44 cohort: On average men in this age bracket save £2,613.82 per year, compared to the £1,398.96 saved by women – a difference of 87% (£1,214.85).

At the younger end of the spectrum, Gen Z savers have the smallest gender savings gap of only 4% (£49.87), with both genders saving roughly the same amount on average per annum: -£1,367.35 for men and £1,317.48 for women.

It's not that we don't want to save. We do. More than men do. It's that we can't save as much.

Statistics show that women are more inclined to save than men but the reality of pay gaps and other structural issues means that the amount we can save is less.

One study[217] shows that women are slightly more likely than men to have savings - 73% of women compared with 71% of men.

This pattern shows up again in data for holdings of individual savings accounts (ISAs), where slightly more women than men are paying into ISAs, but for women 82% of these are cash ISAs compared with 76% for men. (The composition of ISAs is crucially important and we will come to that in the next chapter.)

So while we are more inclined to save, our savings are worth less. One of the factors that comes into play here is having children.

A study conducted on behalf of the Fawcett Society[218] found that the saving behaviour - the inclination and /or ability of men and women to save - was similar until the birth of a first child. 46% of women and 45% of men were saving. That changes when the couple have a child. Unsurprisingly both genders save far less, but, after just one year, 42% of men are still managing to save while only 34% of women are doing so. This difference continues - ten years after the birth, 46% of men are saving compared with 40% of women. The motherhood penalty shows itself again.

The cumulative, compounding effect of these lost savings will be very significant over time.

The US angle

The graph below[219] shows that on every metric apart from having zero savings, women are lagging behind men in the US. This isn't surprising given all the gaps we've already examined but it's stark and troubling. Over 50% of women in the survey had zero savings compared to 39% of men. 23% of women had less than $1,000 saved compared to 25% of men. In every other category up to $50,000 and above, men are saving more.

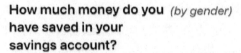

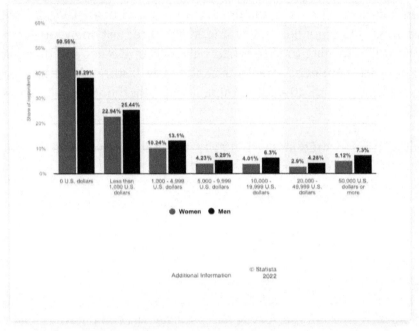

Time to turn that around.

If you have discretionary income, whether a little or a lot, this section will help you save more, and improve your financial health and beyond.

The crucial role played by financial literacy

In a research paper on *perspectives on time* published in 2008,[220] Elizabeth Howlett, Jeremy Keyes and LIA Weir Kemp of Washington State University and the University of New Orleans argue that people are more likely to save for their future pensions if they are "future orientated" and have a greater bias towards thinking about the future *but only if they are in possession of financial knowledge*. Their study found that *if people lacked financial knowledge and know-how* then being future orientated made no difference to their ability to plan, save and invest for the future.

This makes complete sense. If we're not armed with the "how to" aspects of saving and investing for our future then knowing that we should do it is not enough. It's going to be frustrating and disheartening.

That's why financial literacy is so crucial, especially for those who feel excluded from the financial world, where that world talks down to them – women! So share this book. Spread the word, educate your sisters, your daughters, frankly educate everyone.

Who's in control?

Another benefit of improving our financial literacy is that it gives us hope. It helps to feel more in control. That, in itself, can have very positive consequences.

If we flip it around and examine the belief that is quite common (and understandably so) that the cards are stacked against us, that our position is hopeless, this will become a self-fulfilling prophecy as a sense of hopelessness makes any kind of action a waste of time.

Men feel more in control than women

The problem for us is that, disproportionately, women do not feel in control of our finances.

We are twice as likely as men to associate negative emotions with our finances.

In one survey of U.S. adults,[221] almost 40% of women said they feel "overwhelmed" when thinking about their finances and 31% felt "discouraged." Meanwhile, only 9% of women reported feeling "empowered" and only 8% said they felt "excited."

In contrast, men were more likely than women to associate positive feelings with finances. For example, 42% of men reported feeling "in control" of their finances, while 33% felt "hopeful".

The same study showed that twice as many women as men (38% vs. 17%) had less than $400 in total savings, while twice as many men as women (37% vs. 18%) had $50,000 or more in total savings. No wonder men are feeling more hopeful, optimistic and in control than women.

You might say: *there's no point in saving because I don't earn enough...*

I get that, but it's damaging, it's self-perpetuating and it creates a self-fulfilling prophecy.

Psychologists call this the "external locus of control" contrasting it with people who have an "internal locus of control." Research shows that the more likely you are to *feel* that you have an external locus of control, the more likely you *are being controlled* rather than *being in control*.

We need to fight back. The antidote to this is financial literacy, is understanding the external forces that are manipulating us, understanding our own psychology and having a plan.

Get out of my way

Knowing our psyche helps us to challenge it. If we feel we have no control that means any effort to improve our situation is pointless. We are effectively getting in our own way. It is crucial to recognise when our belief systems may be getting in our own way, so we can make them step aside.

If we believe that we have authority and agency in our lives, we improve our positive freedom, allowing us to move forward in all sorts of healthy directions.

Ok, so we believe we have agency, we want to start the process of saving or increase the amount we save, *how do we best move forward?*

- Create a *narrative* that establishes your *goals* and then create a *plan* for how you will achieve that

Many of us are familiar with creating business plans, teaching plans or marketing plans. But how many of us create a financial life plan for ourselves and/or our households? Do we plan, or do we just make it up as we go along?

- Start with a dual narrative. One, crafting the story of *our own ability* to embark on a path that will lead us to our dreams, and two, *identifying* what those dreams and goals might be.

So let's explore and develop that "internal locus of control" I mentioned above. For many of us, our negative, deep seated money biases and inherited money philosophies are ingrained and stubborn and hard to overcome.

If necessary, *fake it till you make it.* This is not a substitute for knowledge but it does help start us on the path to greater financial agency.

- Reframe your own financial identity as a woman who is mastering her relationship with money. Who is in control

Imagine a future you, transformed from someone who is not in control of their finances, to someone who *is* in control. From someone who is not good with money, to someone who *is* good with money. From someone who lives on the hock, to someone who plans. From someone with debts to someone who is debt free. From someone with an uncertain financial future, to someone with a safety net and options, choices and dreams. If your relationship with money is already pretty healthy, imagine how you can make that serve you even better.

- Identify and visualise our dreams

I am also a novelist so I love crafting narratives. Make it big, full bodied and vivid. Deploy all your senses to create a narrative so that you give flesh to your dreams.

Visualising a dream can bring the associated emotions to the forefront - thinking how wonderful being debt-free will feel, how empowering financial independence will feel, how that amazing family holiday will feel, how our grown-up gap year aged 50 will feel, how a second career designed around our passions, not the need to make money, will feel. We can deploy those emotions to help us resist the siren calls of today's emotions calling us to buy *this* or buy *that.*

- Start! And reap the benefits of starting. The wonderful thing about identifying goals is that the mere act of having them helps us on the road to fulfilling them. *Starting them is often the hardest part*

Having established these narratives, we can get into the nitty gritty of making and following the plan and steps necessary to achieving them.

I'm not arguing for miserable austerity. I'm looking for mindful spending where we balance our expenditure with our short, medium and long-term goals.

- Inspire - if we have any young dependents, this will give them a *healthy* template that will inspire them, teach them, and strengthen their own financial health
- Get everyone on board - Family finance

If we are a one-person household then financial planning is much simpler. If we have a partner and/or dependents whether they be children, aged parents or siblings within our household then it can be much more complicated.

- Break the money taboo

It's essential that everyone is on the same page. This can be difficult where families or couples have differing money philosophies. If one of us is saving and working towards long-term goals and the other is casually spending with no thought for tomorrow, it's undermining, frustrating and damaging.

An honest conversation is essential. Yet money remains one of our greatest taboos. According to a survey in 2018 by YouGov commissioned by Lloyds Bank,[222] 50% of UK adults believe that talking about personal money matters is taboo in everyday conversation, higher than for sex (42%), religion (26%) or politics (14%).

We need to break this money taboo for all our sakes. If we talk to our children, and establish healthy saving/spending patterns which we discuss with them, we can endow them with healthy financial habits that will go into their own subconscious and will be influencing them long after we have let go of the literal and metaphoric reins.

- Start Young - Children and money

It's very important to talk to children about money from an early age. Research reveals that our attitudes to money are formed before the age of 7 and above the age of 3.[223]

Personal note:

I remember learning one of my first lessons about money from my mother, who was driven in frustration to share some home truths.

We used to go on mother-daughter shopping outings to Cardiff, stocking up on food at the fruit and vegetable markets, occasionally diverting to the department stores to have coffee and a cake, sometimes just to look.

I couldn't understand why my mother didn't buy me everything I wanted and like most five-year-olds, there were lots of things I wanted. I thought it was extremely unreasonable as all she needed to do was take whatever I wanted to the till, hand over some paper or a piece of plastic and then a nice person behind the till would wrap it up, bag it and hand it over.

It was only when my mother explained about money, that we only had so much, that we would run out, or that we had already run out and we couldn't buy that item that the penny dropped (excuse pun, irresistible!) I remember it very clearly. It made me decide to start saving pennies in a piggybank and shortly after my father opened a bank account for me. All of this had a profound effect on my money education. These lessons and habits were valuable gifts to me.

So, having created our narratives and our goals, how do we set out to achieve them? What can we do both practically and psychologically to help ourselves get there?

First, like anyone navigating using an old-fashioned map, we need to figure out exactly where we are now.

Accounting - Marie Kondo our finances

First of all, we need to do the equivalent of tidying our financial drawers. We need to do some serious accounting to understand what we spend money on, what we need to keep and what needs to go. The number of subscriptions we have that leak money from our account every month is a good place to start.

- Allow your slow brain to make the decisions

Analyse, consider and weigh up. If we analyse where we spend money and see the impact it has on our monthly accounts then we can decide to be more mindful about it. It's binary: *does it help or hinder? Essential or not?*

Do we really need it, or would we be just as happy without it and even happier if we saved that money for our future?

These are thoughtful decisions that we make using our rational brain. Unfortunately quite a few of our spending decisions are made on the hoof, impulsively.

- Beware the fast brain

Think slow guru Daniel Kahneman identified two modes of thinking for the brain associated with different parts of the brain.

One, the fast thinking, relates to the old part of the brain, the lizard brain, the brain that deals with emotions and has evolved over thousands of years to help us make superfast decisions that help save our lives, like: *friend or foe?* or *is that an animal I can eat or will it eat me?* This old brain needed to make snap decisions. Whereas the cerebral cortex is our more modern brain that developed as civilisation and we evolved. This is the rational brain. But it is very often drowned out by the louder, quick acting, impulsive old brain.

How many of you have seen something online, thought to yourself *ooh, I want that,* and bought it in under a minute? I can't be alone in this...

- Protect ourselves from temptation and armour ourselves against the fast brain

We are bombarded 24/7 with marketing emails from companies whose websites we have signed up to.

These are designed to tempt us with beautiful images and sometimes, particularly seductive to me, with *sale* or *discount* offers. This adds urgency and fuel to the fiery urge to *buy now*

These work particularly well on me, if for whatever reason, I'm feeling low or perhaps have had several glasses of wine.

But is this *thing* the solution to feeling down? Is hitting *buy now* the solution? How expensive are these dopamine hits?

- Unsubscribe

When emails flood into my inbox bringing with them the temptation to spend on "stuff" with a few "essential" exceptions, I simply hit *unsubscribe* and temptation vanishes from my inbox, just like that.

Unsubscribing reduces the temptation but temptation is still out there *so how do we fight that?*

How can I protect myself against impulse shopping?

- Pause

If I can escape that website, or Instagram and busy myself with hoovering for 10-minutes, or go for a walk or engage in some mindful breathing, I can deploy my slow, rational brain to ask the questions that I set out above. This doesn't protect me from all impulse buying but it will help me resist the attempts of my emotional brain to hijack me.

So that's a bit more about *how not to spend* but how about *how to save?* What is the optimum way to channel our money into savings?

Understand the endowment effect and the possession principle

There is a psychological phenomenon which means that we are very reluctant to let go of what we already possess. It's called the *endowment effect.*[224] It's effectively a version of a bird in the hand... We can apply it to our money. To our savings, to help make us hang on to them rather than spend them. We don't want to go all Scrooge here and take it to the limit but the principle is a sound one. The trick is to create the savings in the first place so we actually have something we want to protect.

- To save without pain and to boost savings, set up a direct debit every month so that the money is gone before you even see it.

Historical note

Back in the 1940's, the largely unknown but brilliant innovator, Sir Paul Chambers, changed the taxation system, bringing in Pay As You Earn - PAYE. Previously, people had paid tax in arrears, working out what they owed and then signing a cheque to the taxman. Chambers worked out that if you deducted payment directly before it actually got to the recipients, it hurt much less, on the basis of *we don't miss what we never had!*

The psychology at work here is highlighted by the fact that one of the most unpopular taxes ever, the council tax (and also its predecessor the poll tax) is a tax where we see and we feel the money leave our account.

The lesson here is not to rely on informal, spontaneous saving as it hurts more and we are consequently less likely to do it than if the money were removed by an automatic deduction as soon as it hit our main account.

- Take a ride in the sidecar

The government instigated pension auto enrolment policy operates on this principle and the government is now considering creating what they call "sidecar" saving plans which deduct certain amounts of employees' income every month to put into a savings scheme. Tesco and Timpson already offer this to their employees with great success and the government wants to roll this out.

- Get nudged

A version of this operates in the United States and has seen millions of individuals boost their savings. It is based on *nudge theory* saving, where a small, incremental push in the right direction can have strongly positive results. It was initiated by behavioural economist and Nobel prize-winning winner Richard Thaler, together with Schlomo Benarzi. The program is entitled SMarT (*Save More Tomorrow)* and it has 15 million Americans involved in saving. Very cleverly, it does not annex money today but establishes the principle of annexing money tomorrow, siphoning off a portion of future pay rises into retirement savings accounts but leaving take-home pay today unaffected and thus avoids the twin problems of the "loss aversion" we feel when annexing part of our income *today* to benefits way down the road and the "present bias" which makes us care more about today than something way down the road tomorrow.

- Deploy inertia. Make *can't be bothered* work for you

The fact that we have to sign in and correspondingly sign out of this program channels another psychological trait which is *human inertia.* Once we are in we can't be bothered to cancel.

These human characteristics are reflected in the evidence which reveals[225] that 78% of those offered the plan joined, 80% of those who enrolled stayed with it through their fourth pay rise and the average savings rate for participants increased from 3.5% to 13.6% over the course of 40 months.

We don't have that scheme here in the UK but you can make a pledge of your own to siphon off a percentage of any increase in salary to monthly savings as soon as it occurs.

- Understand our present bias so we can negotiate with it

This "present bias" or *temporal discounting,* where we attach greater weight to today than to tomorrow, has a massive effect on our ability to save. Time plays funny tricks on us. Tomorrow feels very different to today and the gap between them distorts our decision-making. Let me give you an example.

Personal note:

Some years back I got into the habit of accepting professional or personal commitments way down the line in the future that I would have rejected out of hand were they to happen tomorrow. Somehow, down the line, they seemed less real and less onerous.

So I developed a psychological trick. I imagined waking up in the morning knowing that the particular commitment was going to happen that very day. Would my spirits soar or plummet? I got a very clear answer and it has helped simplify my life immensely and improve it along the way.

Maybe we can do the same with our money. Imagine waking up into 20 years with a nicely invested pot of savings that we have harvested by not spending today, and tomorrow.

So how do we access this desire to provide for our future self?

- Deploy time metrics to get closer to our future selves

Another temporal hack that psychologists have unearthed is to measure "time metrics." A fascinating study by Dafna Oyserman and Neil Lewis[226] showed that we can connect more strongly to our future selves if we talk in terms of days instead of years, for example looking at retiring in 10,950 days instead of 30 years. If we do that their study finds we start planning for our financial future four times sooner than we otherwise would. So the upshot of this is:

- Convert your time horizons into days

Of course it helps if we are good at delaying gratification. This is something that we could seek to help our children with as studies have shown that children who can exercise willpower so that they are better able to defer gratification tend to do better in life, are happier, and are less likely to fall prey to addictions.[227]

Your present self versus your future self

There is a very clever advertisement that channels behavioural economics that I noticed popping up in national newspapers in spring 2021[228] which shows an older woman on the train looking in the window at the reflection of her younger self. The older woman thanks her younger self for saving and investing to provide for her current self. There is an equivalent for a man looking in the mirror at his younger self whilst wearing a snazzy suit in a tailor's shop.

When we spend, we essentially give our money that we would have to live on later to someone else.

We take away from our future selves and give to strangers.

Personal note

Recently I went into a crystal shop and I saw and fell in love with a pair of museum-grade amethyst geodes. I cannot overstate my yearning to buy these but the money I had in my bank account was in no way sufficient. If I had bought them I would have had to have sold shares. I dreamed about these geodes, I lusted after them but I knew I couldn't have them or *shouldn't* have them. The only thing that helped me stop obsessing about them was the thought that if I did buy them I would be giving a big chunk of my future money to the lovely crystal shop proprietor today.

Different bank accounts for different goals

The thing about money is that it's fungible. One bit of money can quickly be used for something that you didn't intend it for. One way to avoid this is to set up a specific bank accounts for different designated uses. Your salary comes into one which could then pay out a certain amount to the necessities monthly account, another to the monthly capital spending account, another to the savings account and another to the investment account.

Income streams, saving streams, investing streams, guilt free streams and investing streams. All of the above can have their corresponding bank accounts.

Cash Envelopes

Another way is to have cash envelopes where you store physical banknotes which you can spend on specified items - restaurants, cinema or theatre, clothes etc.

These different money streams and different locations make it harder to misspend money. It creates discipline at the beginning of the month and makes spending decisions easier and clearer if you can see where you are in regard to your monthly spending limits for different purposes.

Software can help immensely with debt and spending planners. However, if you love the act of writing and reconciling with a pen and paper that's also very powerful and the act of writing can imprint on our brains, sometimes in a more powerful way. Whatever works best for you.

When spending masquerades as saving: comparison shopping and the *Sale Trap*

One area where we might exercise caution is comparison shopping which may lead us to seek out cheaper products which actually do not serve us well. I would add to that the risk that comparisons may make us buy things we otherwise would not have done, just because they are the cheapest and in theory are "saving us money." Another real and present danger that presents itself multiple times a year with screaming banner headlines and come hither looks is the sale trap.

My mother and I found sales irresistible and ended up buying things that we wouldn't otherwise have bought, gulled by the belief that we were actually "saving money."

I would replace guess how much money I just saved with this is how much money I'm proposing spending.

Another money pit can be "extended warranties and other forms of overpriced insurance." For instance, instead of insuring my mobile phone against damage by dropping it or accidentally breaking it in some way, I buy a big, clunky, bright orange rubberised case which means I can drop the phone on a regular basis, which I do, and it is untroubled, as am I.

One surefire way to save money is to steer clear of brands. The companies involved have spent a lot of money on creating that brand. It does not necessarily mean that they are any, if at all, better than cheaper, less advertised, less branded or even unbranded versions. Sometimes you are literally just paying for their advertising and branding budget.

However, so effective is this branding in manipulating our psyches that we sometimes buy things because they are reassuringly expensive. One study of 800 women taking aspirin, sometimes branded, sometimes unbranded, found that roughly a third of the pain relief the women experienced could be linked to their belief that they were taking the branded drug.[229] This, you might say, is harmless, and in and of itself it is, but if we buy into the whole branded ethos and feel reassured when we pay more for a whole range of products across the board that will seriously impact our spending and hinder our ability to save. Another case for checking our biases and making our belief systems work for us, and not against us.

To sum up:

We are saving less than men even though we feel more inclined than men to save. Having children hits us disproportionately hard when it comes to saving. The role of financial literacy here is, as always, enormous. If we know what to do then we can actually start. Then we can deploy a huge raft of psychological hacks to work powerfully for us (rather than against us as they can sometimes do) and we can turn them into specific savings practices.

What governments can do:

As well as all the earlier suggestions which will also help here, governments can:

- Promote financial literacy
- Roll out the sidecar project across the economy
- Help to alleviate the cost of living crisis where possible by measures such as increasing fuel subsidies, and waiving TV licenses for the poorest households

What companies can do:

- Offer employees sidecars – automatic, pre-agreed saving schemes

What we can do:

- Boost your financial literacy
- Get to know your spending/saving psychology and make it work for you
- Recognise the importance of creating positive emotions around your finances
- Get out of your own way and set aside negative philosophies that

block you
- Frame/reframe your financial identity as a woman who is mastering her relationship with money. Who is in control
- Visualise your dreams
- Create a plan for how to get there
- Befriend your future self
- Use hacks such as time metrics to help
- Calculate the true cost of spending - the number of extra hours you would have to work in order to buy something, and the opportunity cost of giving the money you could have saved and invested for your future self to a random stranger
- Save it before you see it - set up a direct debit so your savings are annexed before they even register in your spending account
- If your employer has a sidecar saving scheme, join it! And stay in it by making inertia work for you
- Start! Starting is the hardest part
- Be aware of the repercussions of having children on your personal saving practices and your ability to save
- Have discussions with your partner to make this as fair and equitable as possible for each of you
- Marie Kondo your finances
- Break the taboo and talk about money in your family
- Inspire and endow your children with healthy financial habits.
- Use apps to help you budget
- Set up different bank accounts
- Use cash envelopes
- Beware of the sales trap
- Ditch branded goods
- Be ruthless in your spending decisions – does it help or not
- Pause
- Deploy your slow brain
- Beware the fast brain
- Protect yourself from temptation – unsubscribe

Save more, work less, slow the treadmill.

Chapter Ten: Women and investing

How to invest better

- In the UK there is a £15 billion gender investment gap[230]

- Women hold £14.3 billion in investments, men hold £29.3 billion

- 21% of men have stocks and share ISAs. Only 13% of women do.

- On average men have £36,000 in their ISA compared to women's £23,000.

- In every age range more women are putting their money into ISAs than men. 11,439,000 women compared to 10,594,000 men.

- That's 8.5% more women subscribing than men. In the age range under 25, 14% more ISA accounts were opened by women than by men.

- **But** 74% of the women who put their money into an ISA in 2017-18 kept it in cash, while only 64% of men put their money in cash

- EToro's female investors increased by 366% in 2021 compared to a 248% increase in men signing up.

- European investment platform Bux saw a 600% increase in women signing up compared to a 400% increase in men signing up.

- But stock market investing remains overwhelmingly the preserve of men. E Toro's clients are 85% men, 15% women, Interactive Investor's 70% men, 30% women, and Hargreaves Lansdowne's 66% men and 33% women.

- Warwick Business School studies showed women investors outperforming the FTSE 100 index and outperforming men

- The women outperformed the FTSE 100 by an annual 1.94%. Men by 0.14%

- Hargreaves Lansdowne showed women outperforming men by an average 0.81% over a three-year period.

- A pattern which if continued for 30 years, would give an average woman a portfolio worth 25% more than the average man.

- If your great-great-grandmother had invested one dollar in the US stock market in 1900, by end 2019, that would be worth $70,000.

- If she'd invested a pound in the UK stock market in 1900, that would be worth £40,000 in 2020.

- **Capital earns more than labour**

- The average home in the UK in 2021 rose in value by £27,000. The average worker earned just under £26,000

When we save, we amass capital which we can then invest to work for us while we sleep.

Capital - definition - wealth in the form of money or other assets

This capital can be the fruits of our labour, or the fruits of existing capital.

Typically, the returns on capital exceed the returns on labour. For example, in the UK in 2021, houses earned more than the typical worker. The average home in the UK in 2021 rose in value by £27,000 while the average worker earned just under £26,000. Your house as well as homing you has out-earned you.

This is particularly relevant for us because as we've seen in the previous chapters, in general, the money coming in is less than it would be if we were men.

So, if we can deploy genderless assets to work for us, we can go some way towards redressing that. There is a wrinkle here though in that in the buying or selling of those genderless assets and the funding thereof we do come into contact with gendered human beings which does impact our profit and loss account. We shall return to that.

The crucial point here is, if the rewards of our labour are not what they should be, let's make our capital work harder for us today. Let's make it work while we eat, sleep, or play.

And do we? Are we? The answer is again that in some areas, we still have ground to make up.

The gender investment gap

In the UK, there is a £15 billion gender investment gap.[231] Women hold £14.3 billion in investments while men hold £29.3 billion.

Alice Moss, managing director for qualitative research at Kantar TNS, observed: "We found that there is a fundamental difference between women and men's levels of self-esteem and financial autonomy. Women can feel embarrassed about their perceived lack of knowledge of the subject and talk about it less frequently with their peers; they also have less connection with the language and marketing used by financial organisations, and have too many other priorities which push investing off their list. They're also not helped by the fact that the sector has been slower than other industries in connecting with a female audience, boosting their self-esteem and reassuring them that they will not be judged."

We've seen that in Anne Boden's campaign *Make Money Equal* which highlights how poorly the financial service industry connects with women.

The gender investment gap is costing us

This gender investing gap shows up strongly in investments made via one of the most potent tools for growing our money - ISAs - Individual Savings Accounts. All gains and dividend income made on stock market investments within ISAs are tax free. This (along with investing in our pensions) is the best way of investing for our future that exists. You can tailor the risk level to suit you and stock market investments are typically liquid meaning you can sell them quickly if you need to, unlike, for instance, investments in property. But yes, their prices are volatile in that they can go up and down. (See *10 Things Everyone Needs to Know About Money* for more on this.)

As of October 2019, 21% of men have stocks and share ISAs whereas only 13% of women do. Not only that, on average men have £36,000 in their ISA compared to women's £23,000.[232]

Now, this isn't because women are profligate and don't want to save.

We are more likely to save in ISAs than men.

In the 2017 to 2018 tax year, government figures show that in every age range more women are putting their money into ISAs than men.

In that tax year, a total of 11,439,000 women subscribed to an ISA compared to 10,594,000 men. That's 8.5% more women subscribing than men. What's particularly interesting is that in the age range under 25, 14% more ISA accounts were opened by women than by men.

But we're not deploying those savings as well as we could

74% of the women who put their money into an ISA in 2017-18 kept it in cash (which is better than the previous year's 80%) whereas only 64% of men put their money in cash, with 29% choosing the stocks and shares ISA (the remainder doing a combination of the two).

This preference for cash is typically why the value of ISA accounts is lower for women than for men. In 2017-18 men's ISA investments were worth on average 11% more than women's. And that's just after one year. When you look at the effect of compounding this preference for cash becomes very expensive over time. Sometimes the greatest risk is to take no risk at all.

Women are increasingly entering the arena

Government stats show that in 2019 to 2020, women accounted for 52% of all ISAs and 50% of ISA holdings worth £50,000 or more.

And more of us are engaging with the stock market. March 2021 saw record trading volumes on various platforms, partially boosted by the whole GameStop speculative phenomenon. EToro said that the number of new female investors in 2020 increased by 366% compared to a 248% increase in men signing up.[233] European investment platform Bux saw a 600% increase in women signing up to its trading app compared to a 400% increase in men signing up. But, despite this, we do not engage with the stock market anything like to the same extent as men. E Toro's client base is 85% men 15% women, Interactive Investor's base is 70% men 30% women and Hargreaves Lansdown which is the U.K.'s largest platform Is 66% men 33% women.

Historical note

Women have been investing in the stock market since the 1600s. Some women did it for fun, some women did it to supplement the "pin money" given them by their husbands as an allowance to buy fripperies. Never enough to run away with but enough to tide us over if we were lucky with fripperies like ribbons and toiletries. But even that was considered dangerous. An article by Addison in The Spectator of February 7th 1712 cautioned husbands against giving their wives pin money, suggesting that those who did would be "furnishing her with arms against himself, and in a manner becoming accessory to his own dishonour."

The implication here is clear: if you give money to women, if you help them become independent, they will dishonour you. Therefore, to control women, control their access to money.

But, rebellious, canny women, some rich, some not, discovered back in the sixteen hundreds and thereafter, an invisible way to make money which escaped the notice of their husbands or their fathers or society at large:

They invested in the stock market.

Women like Sarah Duchess of Marlborough recently immortalised in the film *The Favourite*. Sarah was an active purchaser of stocks. In 1725 she owned £36,500 worth of shares. She couldn't vote in parliamentary elections but she could invest in the stock market. Far more humble women also invested.

The market allowed women to hold very small amounts[234]. Theodasia Neal from Northamptonshire owned book value of £10 of stock. There was a wonderful democracy at work here. shareholdings gave women across the ranks of society (admittedly not the poorest who most needed it) a safety net. it gave them a nest egg and a small stream of dividend income. Something that was theirs and theirs only, on which they could rely.

As C. Ingrassia notes: "stock jobbing allows women to transcend, however briefly, constraints and their activities and increase their knowledge, discretionary income and power." Amen to that. Then and now.

Investing did not meet with universal acclaim. W.D. MacDonald wrote in his tract, Fraud on the Widow's share,[235] that "no thought is given to the possibility – indeed the probability – that the widow will be inexperienced in money matters and the lump sum will soon be dissipated."

What these commentators are saying is: don't trust women with money because not only will they behave badly and bring dishonour upon you but they will lose it all!

Looking at women investors today W. D. McDonald would have ended up with egg on his face.

For here's an inconvenient truth: when women do invest, we can be rather good at it. *In fact better than men.*

Women with the Midas touch

Warwick Business School analysed 2,800 UK men and women investing with Barclays' Smart Investor over three years.[236] Their results showed that the women outperformed the FTSE 100 index and outperformed the men.

The women outperformed the FTSE 100 by an annual 1.94%. Men by 0.14%.

A separate study by Hargreaves Lansdowne[237] reinforced these findings. Women outperformed men by an average 0.81% over a three-year period. Hargreaves observes that if this pattern continued for 30 years, the average woman would end up with a portfolio worth 25% more than the average man.

Our US sisters are similarly excelling.

Fidelity Investments analysed a sample of its 5 million customers over ten years and found that, on average, women outperformed their male counterparts by 0.4%.[238] That might not sound like a lot but as in the Hargreaves Lansdowne study cited above, the compounding effect of this really adds up.

Why do female investors outperform their male counterparts?

Boys will be Boys: Gender, Overconfidence and Common Stock Investment.

One of the earliest, and without doubt the best-named study, took place in the US. In 2001, the Massachusetts Institute of Technology published a report called "Boys will be Boys: Gender, Overconfidence and Common Stock Investment."[239] The authors analysed trading activity in over 35,000 households, comparing men and women. They discovered that men trade more frequently than women and do so from a false faith in their own financial acumen. Intriguingly, they discovered that single men traded less sensibly than married men and married men traded less sensibly than single women.

Also, according to Marina Lui from Swiss bank UBS Asia wealth unit,[240] "women are more likely to invest in ways that preserve wealth for their offspring, while the overriding focus for men is investing for higher instant returns."

The one thing we do know is that the stock market does not provide instant or even near instant gratification. If that is one of your motivations you're going to get hammered by volatility (prices going up, down, up down, sometimes dizzyingly).

The fact that women take a longer-term view means that we trade less frequently. The Warwick study observed that while women investors traded on average 9 times each year, men traded on average 13 times. There are two issues here. One is trading costs. Each time you trade, it costs you in transaction fees. Over time, these costs erode returns. The second issue is with market timing. Trying to time the market, the perfect time to buy and sell, is almost impossible and tends to backfire.

Another factor is that women tend to gravitate towards typically less risky investments with a more consistent performance history while men gravitate to riskier Investments with potentially higher returns, a form of "investment thrill seeking." The Warwick study found that women were more likely to invest in funds rather than the individual stocks favoured by men, and in doing that we have been diversifying our portfolio, reducing risk and typically leading to fewer losses.

So women, let's get investing. Let's take a closer look at what investing in the stock market can give us and then how to do it.

Let's start with why we don't so that we can address that and overcome it.

Many of us choose not to invest in the stock market for two main reasons.

1) The stock market looks terrifying.

Newspaper articles and TV news have seared our consciousness by showing the occasional massive falls in the market. The effects of the pandemic saw many stock markets around the world drop by 30% in March 2019. Since then however, they have more than recovered. More recently, as well as causing humanitarian tragedies, the invasion of Ukraine by Russia has caused large fluctuations in stock markets. From an investor standpoint, you need to be able to take a long-term view.

2) We don't understand it

The other thing that puts us off is the perception that we just don't understand the market and because we don't understand it we cannot invest in it.

I know this might sound heretical, but you don't need to understand it to any great depth to be able to invest in it. You might think that you need to be an expert in predicting the movements of shares before you dare touch it, but let me tell you, even the professionals have a mixed record in trying to predict it. Some observers call the movement of the stock market "a random walk."

You don't need to understand it.

You just need to understand the process of how to invest in it, what to look out for and what to avoid. You need to be able to find some good funds run by a good fund manager or even just buy some tracker funds composed of weighted components of stock market indices which track those indices up and down. I write about these in more detail in *10 Things Everyone Needs to Know About Money* but I will cover them in part in the how-to section below.

Most people trying to get rich quick via the stock market will get burned and will instead get poor quick.

However, slow investing pays dividends, both literally and metaphorically.

Get rich slow - the antidote to terrifying plunges in the market

Once you have invested in the stock market via a good fund or an index, you need to sit back and resist the temptation to check your portfolio on anything more frequent than a monthly basis. The nature of volatility, of ups and downs, means that you will severely stress, or even terrify yourself if you look at performance over the short term. Psychologists have shown the pain of losses is about 2 ½ times more powerful than the pleasure of wins and so you need to look to the long term to get the wins and to get the associated pleasures, not to mention the financial security boosts that go with them. You need to look to the long term: 7 or 10 or ideally 15 or 20 years.

You might ask, *why would I want to invest in the stock market given that it looks terrifying and I don't understand it? Why should I go to that trouble? What's so special about equities (shares)?*

The short answer is, because if you want your money to grow, equities are a heck of a lot better than keeping your money in cash, or buying treasury bills or longer-term bonds.

The Credit Suisse Global Investment returns Yearbook of 2021[241] report reveals that over the past 120 years in the USA, equities increased in value on average by 9.7% every year.[242] In the UK equities did almost as well increasing on average by 9.1% every year.[243]

What this boils down to is this: if your great-great-grandmother had invested one dollar in the US stock market in 1900, that would be worth just under $70,000 by the end of 2019, or $40,000 if you stripped out the effect of inflation (which increased by 3000% over that period).

If the same great-great grandmother had invested a pound in the UK stock market in 1900, that would be worth just under £40,000 in 2020. That is the power of long-term equity market investments.

Unsurprisingly equities outperformed bonds and Treasury bills. We would expect to see this as higher returns go with higher risk and equities are riskier than bonds and bonds are in turn riskier than Treasury bills/cash.

You may say that actually you don't have 120 years to play with but luckily don't need that long.

Let's look at the magic of compound returns.

The time value of money - Compound Returns, Einstein's Eighth Wonder of the World

Let me share with you the example of a humble American man called Ronald Read. Read repaired cars at a petrol station for 25 years and cleaned floors at JCPenney for 17 years. When he was 38 he bought a two-bedroom house for $12,000 and he lived there all his life. He died in 2014 at 92 years of age. He left a staggering $8 million in his will. He didn't win the lottery. He didn't have a surprise inheritance. Read's secret was that he saved what he could and invested it in high quality "blue chip" shares. Then he sat back and allowed compounding to work its magic until in the end his investments were worth over $8 million.

That, my friends, is the power of compounding.

What this example shows is that you don't need to start off rich to end up rich.

If you can buy a cappuccino every day then you're rich enough to invest.

Cappuccino economics and the joys of compounding

Small savings can grow into substantial sums if you invest regularly and you start young, as Ronald Read demonstrated.

Let's say you forego your daily £3.50 cappuccino and invest the money instead in a low-cost diversified equity fund. What would you say if I told you that in 30 years you could have a portfolio worth £105,000?

Here's the maths:

- Monthly savings: £105
- Investment frequency: monthly
- Average return: 6%
- Value in 30 years: £105,474

Let's change the model slightly to show the power of regular investing. Let's assume that instead of investing £105 every month you filled a jam jar until you had an annual pot of £1260 and you invested that once a year for 30 years.

The future value comes out at £99,613. So you lose out on roughly £6,000 just because you invest annually rather than monthly.

Maybe your time horizon is 10 years so let's look at what might happen if we invest £150 a month for a decade with a 6% compounding rate. After 10 years your nest egg would be just under £25,000. That compares to a nest egg of £18,000 if you'd stuck it under the mattress.

It's not quite so exciting is it, not such a big gap. What this reveals is that the more time you can give compounding to work, the better.

If you have children, teach them about compound returns and if possible show them.

Investing for your children

As of 2021, you can put up to £9000 in a junior stocks and shares or cash

ISA each year.

If you want to save for your children's university education or perhaps for a deposit on a home one day, long-term equity investments offer much better hope than cash. A National Savings and Investments Junior ISA only pays 3.4%, as we've seen above, even with the recent increase this is much less than you would typically get on investing in the stock market, particularly if you add to the compounding power by reinvesting dividends.

I'll give you an example of the benefits of reinvesting dividends. Sometimes the stock market indices "go sideways." This means that the value of the index can remain stubbornly stuck. Let's look at a historical example. If you invested £1,000 on New Year's Eve 1999 in the FTSE 100 and then sat on it, by the 14th of December 2018 that £1,000 investment would have decreased to £993 if you had not reinvested dividends.[244] But, if you had reinvested dividends, your investment would have risen to £1,935 by December 2018. That's an annual return of 3.54% compared with -0.04 percent if you'd invested in the index alone. [245]

The case sounds compelling for investing our savings into the stock market doesn't it?

But most parents, 70% of us, save for our children's future in cash. Only 30% invest our children's savings. That is particularly worrying in periods of inflation. Post pandemic, we have seen inflation rise from practically nothing to 6% and rising in the UK and many economists fear that the spectre of inflation will haunt us for many years to come. Inflation erodes the purchasing power of cash but, in general, the stock market will increase ahead of inflation, or at least mitigate its effects and will offer us far greater protection than cash.

Pensions for our children

Sounds a bit mad doesn't it, having a baby and imagining their 67 year old self but their 67 year-old self will thank you richly if you or their grandparents do set up a pension for them. Currently, as of February 2022 you can invest up to £2,880 into a Junior Self Invested Personal Pension for under 18s. HMRC bumps this up by 20% up to a total of £720 making a potential annual investment total of £3600. This would enable compounding returns to do their magic over a 50 to 60 year period.

£3,600 invested annually for 60 years at an assumed compounding rate of 6% would give a lump sum of Just under £2 million![246] If you bump the annual return up to 8% that would yield just over £4.5 million pounds.

Given that the Credit Suisse Global Investment returns Yearbook of 2021[247] report reveals that over the past 120 years in the USA, equities increased in value on average by 9.7% every year[248] and in the UK by an average by 9.1% every year, those figures are not unrealistic.[249]

It's worth noting that a Junior Sipp allowance comes on top of a Junior ISA allowance so if you're able you could save money into both up to a limit of £9,000 annually.

So, how do we invest in the stock market?

Stock market investing: how to

1) The first thing you need is to find an investment platform. Think of this as a shopfront through which you can actually invest. Platform fees vary considerably. Some of them charge flat annual fees and some charge per transaction. Have a look at our helpful resources at the end to see further advice on how to pick a platform.
2) Always plan to invest as much as possible via an ISA so that any gains and dividends from your investments will be tax-free. Annual allowances for individuals are now £20,000. The investing platform Hargreaves Lansdown has some very good advice with regard to the mechanics of investing via an ISA.
3) Next you need to pick your specific investment. I very rarely pick individual shares. I much prefer to pick a good fund manager (see helpful resources again back) and then a fund which will invest in a range of different companies. This is the principle of diversification a.k.a. not putting all your eggs in one basket.

An alternative way to invest is to get yourself a financial adviser but unless you have at least £50,000 to invest this will not give you a bang for your buck as typically you might get the first consultation free and then if you take their advice you will likely be charged between 1% and 3% of your investable assets (according to Quilter.) On top of that you'll be charged a yearly fee of between half and 1%. Some of the large investment platforms such as Hargreaves Lansdown and AJ Bell offer you free guidance. You pay to trade by their platforms but you can read their advice for free.

One of the cheapest ways to invest in the stock market is via what is known as a tracker fund.

Tracker funds - Why look for needles when you can buy the whole haystack?

Trackers are essentially a weighted portfolio of shares which aim to track the performance of various indices, such as the FT 100 or the S&P 500. So, if the index goes up by 5% a year, your tracker fund will go up by 5% a year and correspondingly if it goes down by 5% a year your investment will go down by 5% a year. They are a cheap way of investing[250] and they offer you a great degree of diversification particularly if you purchase different indices in different countries such as the UK, US. The founder of investment giant Vanguard, Jack Bogle famously said: "why look for needles when you can buy the whole haystack?"

The stock market is in many ways the easiest and best way that we can invest but let's look at a range of other options as well.

The main asset classes that we can invest in are apart from the stock market are:

- Cash under the mattress
- Cash in a bank or building society
- Bonds
- Other financial investments such as bitcoin
- Gold in the form of shares in a gold company or gold coins or slivers of gold. Same for silver.
- Property
- Land
- Forestry

- Fine wines
- Casked whisky
- Stamps
- Art
- And...handbags!

The lure of cash and the risk of going broke slowly

Cash is wonderful. Dostoevsky called money "coined liberty" and it is just that. Up to a point. As we saw earlier, many of us are over-enamoured with holding our savings in cash. This sounds sensible and prudent but taken too far we expose ourselves to what is known as *reckless conservativism,* and we face the very real prospect of going broke slowly.

The trouble with cash is that interest rates, even though they have recently started to rise from their all-time lows (in some countries turning negative) are still low. Lower than inflation. Which is rising, Predicted to hit 8% in 2022. Inflation erodes the value of your cash given that it exceeds the level of interest rates (meaning that the real interest rate is negative.) This means that what your cash will actually buy grows less and less every year.

Having said all that, cash is still extremely important and has its place in every financial portfolio for several reasons.

The case for cash

Cash is a security blanket, a safety net, something you need to have in your portfolio for when time gets tough. Covid taught us that when things go wrong they can go very wrong. We could lose our jobs, we could see a big reduction in our income even if we're lucky enough to keep our jobs, and our businesses could be pummelled.

The typical advice is to keep six months' worth of expenditure as cash, mostly in the bank but also keep some physical cash at home. Immediate access to cash is always important as it protects us against being locked out of our bank or any other cyber issues that might arise.

The wonderful thing about cash is that it gives us options. Morgan Housell in his brilliant book *The Psychology of Money*[251] notes that even when interest rates are negative, there is a conceptual, psychological return on cash which doesn't appear in the hard maths.

If having cash enables you not to sell equities, especially into a falling market, allowing the compounding that I've spoken of earlier to work its magic, then cash should be attributed with a conceptual return that will deliver very tangible effects on your investment portfolio.

It also correspondingly enables you to buy in falling markets, taking advantage of the sudden discounts.

When the markets were pummeled by lockdowns, many commentators described it as *the buying opportunity of a generation*. That sounds vulture-like but the truth of it is we're not actually harming anyone by buying into those falling markets.

There is also another scenario where having cash is invaluable. As *running away* money. For women who wish to escape from a violent, abusive partner, cash can be a lifeline. We look at that in more detail in Chapter 11.

The value of a good night's sleep

Having cash can help you sleep at night and as we all know that is incredibly important to our overall health and sanity.

Bonds

Investing in bonds is best done via diversified funds run by fund managers who almost all have bond allocations in their portfolios. This is not a market for the individual investor for a whole host of reasons.

Property

This is the biggie. The asset that just keeps on giving. Our home, our haven and normally a spectacular investment over time as anyone lucky enough to own property already knows. Our home typically does not count as an investment unless we wish to downsize in the future, which many of us do. The fact remains that property tends to be an extremely good long term investment, particularly if we are able to borrow money to finance our home at a lower interest rate than the prevailing rate of property price inflation. I write more about this with a specific example in *10 Things Everyone Needs to Know about Money*.

Forestry

Wonderful but a tad obscure to detail here.

Gold

Keen investors in gold are known as goldbugs. Central Banks always hold healthy reserves of gold which they keep as a war chest or a safe haven in times of crisis. Many investors who fear inflation turn to gold as it has reliably protected and preserved the real value of their money. To read more about this see my section on hyperinflation in the Weimar Republic of Germany, in *10 Things Everyone Needs to Know about Money*.

The upside of gold is that it is a safe haven for your money much of the time but the downside is that gold can be quite volatile - prices can rise and fall quickly. Also you make no income from gold - there are no dividends as there are on stock market investments, unless you invest in a company involved with mining gold which is one way to get exposure to the precious metal.

One particularly attractive way to invest is to buy gold coins. In the United Kingdom, due to the fact that they are deemed to be currency, they are not liable for capital gains tax which means any increase in their value will be free of tax. They also make wonderful presents and are an antidote in many ways to the consumerism of "stuff" - plastic toys, clothes etc. The Royal Mint has a wide range of silver and gold coins for sale which would make wonderful presents.

Get wasted!

Another tax-free way to invest is via what are called "wasting assets" - defined by HMRC as an asset with a predictable life of 50 years or less. The most well-known wasting assets are wine and whisky.

And the thing is, their value does tend to appreciate.

Wine has performed well over time. The same goes for whisky.

I've recently bought a couple of casks of whisky. I hope they will prove to increase in value faster than inflation. If everything goes to pot, I can at least barter with them, or drink them...

In a 10 year period (to 2019) in which classic cars went up 258%, coins 193%, and art 158%, the value of rare whisky grew by of 582%.[252]

The power of a good handbag

I've always bridled at clothes or handbags being defined by fashion magazines as "investments". I read this as just an exhortation to make us buy more stuff, but there is another sense in which handbags can be very good investments.

Over the year to 2021, the value of high-end handbags increased by 17%, fine wine by 13%, and classic cars by 6%.[253] Over ten years, prices for bags have more than doubled, with a 108 per cent growth recorded.

Are diamonds really a girl's best friend?

Diamonds, particularly higher grade, can be a useful, and portable, investment.

A 2012 study[254] using data from auctions that between 1999-2010 shows that the annualized real USD returns for white and coloured diamonds was 6.4% and 2.9%, respectively. Since 2003, the average returns have been 10.0%, 5.5%, and 6.8% for white diamonds, coloured diamonds, and other gems, respectively. Both white and coloured diamonds outperformed stocks between 1999 and 2010. However, the study also shows that there is a positive correlation between the level of the stock market and diamond prices. When the stock market rises, so do diamond prices. This is a result of wealth-induced demand for luxury consumption in collectibles markets.

I'm nervous about diamonds in one respect. The prices are kept artificially high by creating a false scarcity. There are bulk holdings of diamonds which are kept locked away in order to create this scarcity. However in certain circumstances I still believe it is worth having diamonds in your physical possession. See later chapter on Women and the Dark Side of

Money.

Historical note

Back in the Russian Revolution which began in 1917, many members of the aristocracy fled the Bolsheviks, very often with just the clothes they were wearing. But… Into the hems of those clothes were stitched diamonds…

Stamps

A survey in Forbes magazine by Richard Lehmann in 2018[255] shows that while stamps have been an interesting investment in the past they have not done particularly well in recent years.

They surveyed around 2700 different stamps, concluding that in the 3 years to 2018, US stamps appreciated 1.3% on average, compared to the average rate for the last 13 years of 2.1% a year). Items valued at over $1000 appreciated at an average rate of 3.2% per year over a 13 year period making them a much better investment than stamps below $1000.

What is emerging from these stats is that it pays to buy quality, it pays to buy the rarer species of whatever it is you're buying, whether it be stamps, diamonds or whisky.

To sum up:

Historically, the returns on capital far exceed the returns on our labour.

Yet there exists a gender investment gap and we need to close that. This can be done by greater self education and a more nuanced understanding of risk. It would also be good if the financial service companies engaged more with women. Belatedly they are waking up towards the (nauseatingly called) *pink pound*.

Women want to save, we are more inclined to save than men.

For centuries women have deployed the transcendent power of the stock market to grow wealth, especially in an era when earning income via a job was not open to us.

Over long periods of time, particularly when dividends are reinvested, investing in the stock market is an excellent way to grow wealth.

When we do invest in the stock market, we tend to out-perform men, partially as a result of not being over confident.

What governments can do:

- Yet again, boost financial literacy
- Raise investing thresholds in line with inflation

What companies can do:

- Connect with women
- Develop a language that speaks to women
- Recruit more female advisors who can help make female potential investors feel more comfortable
- Stop treating women like a homogenous bunch and offer us tailored, nuanced, jargon-free financial advice

What we can do:

- Bolster our financial literacy
- Talk with other women about investing – maybe set up a saving and investment club like a bookclub with a difference
- Recognise the pros and cons of cash
- Recognise the risk of going broke slowly by over-reliance on cash savings
- Invest in the stock market!
- Find a reputable platform
- Find a reputable fund manager
- Pick your funds
- Diversify
- Reinvest dividends
- Use as much of your ISA allowance as possible.
- Turn your reticence and lack of confidence into an investing superpower – the alchemy of humility

- Remember that time in the market beats timing the market
- If you want more support, find yourself a female financial advisor
- get wasted!
- When investing in "alternatives," buy the highest quality you can afford
- Befriend the best diamonds
- Deploy the handbag
- ***Always*** do your homework before investing. See further resources at the end of the book.

Chapter Eleven: Women and money: the dark side

Financial and economic abuse. How to spot it, stop it, escape it

- Financial abuse occurs in all socio-economic, educational, racial and ethnic groups

- It takes place within a context of coercive control

- This is a massively under-reported crime

- It is estimated that in the UK, in 2020 to 2021, as many as 1.5 million victims did not report being coercively controlled

- The implied prosecution rate is an almost invisible 0.1%

- A UK survey reported that 61% of female victims of intimate partner abuse were in debt because of financial abuse

- On average, female survivors of economic abuse carried an average debt of £3,818, compared to men's £2,926

- The abuse lasts longer for women

- Men were more likely than women to say that the abuse lasted for less than 6 months (20% compared to 12%)

- Women were significantly more likely than men to say that the abuse lasted for five years of more (34% compared to 15%)

- In the US, research indicates that financial abuse occurs in 99% of domestic violence cases

- Survivors state that financial concerns were one of the top reasons for staying in or returning to an abusive partner

- In the UK, 89% of women who experienced economic abuse said they also experienced other forms of abuse

- Estimates suggest that financial abuse costs the global economy $15.6 billion every year

Many of the things we've learned and covered in previous chapters will stand us in good stead but there is an extra dimension we need to address when looking at women and money. How to make our money work for us when things go wrong in our own lives, with our supposed 'nearest and dearest.'

There is a dark side of money where we lie about it, where we *need* to lie about it. We all live with moral compromises, with the necessary lies we tell. Sometimes it stems from the desire to protect others, withholding information that would trouble them, other times we are forced to keep secrets for our very survival. That is the darkest side of all.

Financial dishonesty

Let's start with the pale grey. Almost half of us in Britain have money secrets which we do not share with our partners. A survey conducted by the Money and Pension service to mark *Talk Money Week* found that 4 in 10 people kept money secrets.[256] Some cover debt, others conceal secret savings. Those aged between 25 and 34 are apparently the most secretive. Nearly 60% of them have secret credit cards, personal loans and overdrafts. This contrasts with retired people 65 and over who are much more open. Just over 25% of that age group kept financial secrets or at least owned up to it.

It's interesting to note that we tend to underestimate how secretive our partners are with regard to money. 23% of us suspect that our partner keeps money secrets while around 45% of us have money secrets ourselves.

More than 38% of people said that the stigma surrounding talking about money meant they stayed silent about financial worries, fearing embarrassment or being judged.

It's a heavy burden to carry on our own. And it's startling that for whatever reason, so many of us do not trust our partners and feel the need to keep secrets. There is a sliding scale of justification here.

Let's look at the darkest side of money - at one of the reasons why we might like to keep money secrets – coercive control.

With respect to money, this takes two forms:

Economic abuse and financial abuse

We've established that money is intrinsically linked with power. So what better way to exercise power over another individual than to control their money.

A study in Australia[257] estimates that financial abuse cost victims in Australia $5.7 billion in 2020.

Economic and financial abuse affect women's pasts, present and the future.

A survey by Opinium for the Co-op and Refuge in 2020[258] found that as many as 1 in 5 women had experienced financial abuse at some point in their lives. However, due to its hidden nature and the element of control exercised by abusers, the abuse is extremely hard for external agencies to spot. They note that people subject to economic abuse carried debts of £3272 as a result, equivalent to £14.4bn of economic-abuse related debt in the UK.

"Many people don't recognise financial abuse right away, in part, because of historic gender roles," says Sarah Gonzalez Bocinski, director of the US based Institute for Women's Policy Research's Economic Security for Survivors Project.[259]

Economic and financial abuse comes under the umbrella of coercive control which similarly is very difficult to recognise. It is under reported, under recognised, and under punished. In the United Kingdom between April 2020 and September 2021, of the 15,338 coercive control offences reported, just 1,717 people were prosecuted. That represents a prosecution rate of 3.4%. But given the assessment by the Crime Survey of England and Wales which suggests that as many as 1.5 million victims do not report the abuse, the implied prosecution rate is an almost invisible 0.1%. Most victims are unlikely to ever get justice. The issue here is that apart from the terror of those victims having to report it to police, very often the police lack the training to spot what is going on. Farah Nazeer, the Chief Executive of Women's Aid, quoted in an article in *The Daily Telegraph* on 23 April 2022, says that although, "There are lots of good hard working committed police out there, at large the police don't really understand coercive control. They don't understand how to look for evidence, how to ask the right questions, and they are very often convinced by the perpetrator. Unless they have had the rigours of training to understand domestic abuse and coercive control, they can draw the wrong conclusions from the way something initially presents." Unfortunately, so far only two thirds of police forces in England and Wales have signed up to send officers on a course to help identify coercive control and domestic abuse. Not only that, but problems in the criminal justice system are not helping victims. Many perpetrators receive lenient sentences. Nazeer adds, "We are aware that judges are not trained in domestic abuse or violence against women and girls. They misunderstand it, misinterpret it and there is a lot of concern about the sort of lenient sentences being handed down."

So what is it?

Coercive control involves emotional and physical abuse with victims being told how to behave, who they can see, who they must not see and how they spend their time whether inside or outside the home.

Economic and financial abuse are defined as systematic behaviour where one person tries to control another person's access to the means by which they might be able to earn money, or to money itself.

Economic abuse is where somebody stands between you and your ability to further your professional ambitions, limiting your ability to achieve your dreams with all the ensuing financial consequences. This could be a parent stopping their daughter attending sixth form, university or an apprenticeship. It could be a husband preventing his wife from furthering her qualifications or taking a promotion. In many cases it has become normalised behaviour so that the victim doesn't even recognise it as abuse. This makes it much harder for her to take action against it or to seek help. Reducing or controlling her ability to work and earn her own independent money, also makes it harder for her to leave.

A 2020 report by the Co-operative Bank and Refuge[260] found that this form of abuse is widespread: 10% of survey respondents said that their partner would not let them work; 11% said that their partner did things to stop them going to work and 9% said that their partner would not allow them to go to college or university. In addition, 9% said that they worked for their partner, or a family business but they were not paid. Unfortunately, this data was not segregated by gender.

A report in the United States[261] showed that 70% of domestic violence victims are forbidden to work by their abusers.

Historical note

Women have been fighting against this kind of economic abuse for centuries. In 1792, Mary Wollstonecraft (a pioneering feminist immortalised in a somewhat controversial sculpture by Maggie Hamblin) published a book called: "A Vindication of the Rights of Women." In it she argued that under existing educational philosophies and practices, women were educated to be /deliberately trained to be frivolous and incapable. She pushed for radical reform so that girls would be given the same educational advantages as boys. We still see this presumption of frivolity in financial advertisements targeted at women: see Anne Boden's "Make money equal" initiative covered in earlier chapters.

Financial Abuse

Like economic abuse, financial abuse cuts across all sections of society.

And again, many of the victims and their wider families can be either unaware that it's going on, or fail to recognise it as abuse.

Different manifestations of financial abuse:

Interception of post

A Citizens Advice report[262] published in 2020, identified the role of the interception of post in domestic and economic abuse: half of survivors surveyed said that the perpetrator had intercepted their post. This interception would enable the perpetrator to switch ownership of assets into their own name without the victim's knowledge, to access the victim's money and benefits, and to plunge them into debt.

Coerced debt

Coerced debt is defined as 'debt generated through financial transactions which the victim is told to make (or is unaware of the abuser making in their name) in a context where there are negative consequences for non-compliance'.

This could manifest as having sole responsibility for mortgage payments or bill payments. Coercing their victims into debt is one of the most common ways abusers control their victims, because once you have large amounts of debt in your name or a low credit score, it can be difficult to rent an apartment and, in some cases, even get a job.

A study by the Cooperative Bank and Refuge[263] shows the impact of abuse on personal debt.

- 57% of those who had experienced economic abuse said that they were in or had been in debt because of economic abuse
- The average survivor of economic abuse carried £3,272 of coerced debt - equivalent to £14.4 billion of debt across the UK
- A quarter of survivors have debts of over £5,000

The report reveals how it is women who are suffering the most.

- On average, women survivors of economic abuse bore an average debt of £3,818 compared to £2,926
- The abuse lasts longer for women. "Men were more likely than women to say that the abuse lasted for less than 6 months (20% compared to 12%). And women were significantly more likely than men to say that the abuse lasted for five years of more (34% compared to 15%)"

The toxic legacy effect of this can be seen in that: "Women were much more likely to say that they were still paying off debt related to economic abuse at the time of the survey (54% of women, compared to 29% of men)."

The report concludes that: "This combined with the findings on other forms of domestic abuse experienced suggests that women are more likely to experience economic abuse as part of a long-term pattern of controlling and coercive behaviour."

The abuse is not confined to financial. The report also notes that:

- 89% of women who experienced economic abuse said they also experienced other forms of abuse, reporting higher rates of physical, emotional and sexual abuse compared to men

In the US, research[264] indicates that financial abuse occurs in 99% of domestic violence cases. Survivors reflect that financial concerns were one of the top reasons for staying in or returning to an abusive partner.

What these reports show is how women affected are caught in a trap. The very women who most need to leave a relationship are the least able to.

Let's take a specific look at how women can suffer from economic abuse, both those who are dependent on their abuser and those who earn their own money.

Personal note

May's story (name changed).

May is married to a man who has not worked for the last fifteen years despite living the life of an aging rock star including all the usual infidelities and excesses. He survives on her earnings as a freelance cosmetic doctor. Over the years he has encouraged her to trade almost entirely in cash as a supposed tax reduction measure. The cash is secured in the house safe that only he has access to at any time. She has to ask for her own money if she needs any.

The question is how did this happen? I can only explain it by suggesting it's a balance between him being a manipulative con man and a violent bully who has over the years frightened her and eroded her self-esteem and confidence to the extent that she feels unable to leave him. And obviously, the fact that he controls her hard-won assets means she lacks the resources to leave him.

An escape plan for the trapped

I've engaged in long debates with myself as to whether or not to share what I call an "extraction plan" for women who wish to escape from a dangerously abusive relationship. I have decided that I will share it and you will find my suggestions below. This is hard enough for a woman on her own but with children this becomes perilously difficult and dangerous. There are no easy answers here but refuges are likely to be the safest bet. If there is no violence involved then taking the financial measures I suggest to amass your running away funds are still viable.

In May's case it is a matter of protecting her money and controlling who has access to it. In an abusive relationship this can be difficult. One approach might be to do a "Trump" and not declare all earnings. The success of this approach is wholly dependent on securing the audit trail from all but yourself, while at the same time creating solid documentation to support what you are prepared to declare. There may be many ways to do this which will depend on your specific employment circumstances.

So, what could May do about the situation? In order to address this I am going to examine all the means that, let's call him Warren, uses to monitor and control her:

Post

This is a tricky one because May would need to intercept it before Warren does, without him having any idea what she's up to. The old-fashioned method here is best. If May can safely steam open the letters, copy the contents and reseal the letters without arousing Warren's suspicions then she can arm herself with information as to what he's up to.

Social Media

Most small business owners today rely heavily on social media in order to promote their business and to manage their client base. As a result, going quiet on social media is not an option. The solution to this is to keep the social media entirely business and keep a "low flow" on the overt business activity and engage with your client base over other apps such as WhatsApp and Signal where you can control exactly who is in the group and protect your content appropriately. You cannot block him from the social media site for two main reasons: if it is a violent and abusive relationship It will provoke him. Secondly, you will inform him that you are taking action to protect yourself and that will alert him to be more suspicious and scrutinise your day to day activity more directly.

Phone and communications

Don't fall for the "Oh look darling I've bought you a new iPhone just like mine", trick. It is highly likely that the iPhone (or android phone for that matter) will be set up on his account and will be set to automatically back up to his cloud account with either Apple or Google. This means that he has a copy of all your information - data, photographs and if you store your passwords and account details in "notepad" he has them too. That however is not the whole story as by using the "Find My" option (Google has similar) he will be able to track you at any time he wishes. If you are going to have the same type of operating system (phone) as him then ensure that it is registered to your own account and that you have control of the cloud back-up at all times. This comes in useful later on when we discuss escape packs and preparation for extraction.

Ideally have a different type of phone on a different operating system to his. If he has an iPhone, get a Samsung or vice versa. You can defuse any objection by simply saying that you prefer them or just fancy a change. If you are going to save your passwords in notepad, consider "encrypting" them using a simple algorithm known only to you. For example, write out the alphabet and say that every letter is three letters further along, e.g. A becomes C and D becomes F. Upper Case and lower case are inverted and numbers work backwards from 9 to 0. It's easy to make up your own code.

Buy a "clean" phone with a pay as you go SIM commonly known as a "burner phone" where there is no monthly payment required and no incriminating monthly bill. Remember to use the phone occasionally to call yourself and top it up so as to keep the SIM card live and connected. Secure this in your escape pack. Set this phone up on your Apple or Google account as a "New Phone" and sync it so that all your data is set up on the burner phone as it is on your current phone. Then **delete the burner from your account** in case the account or the phone gets compromised. Do this activity monthly or every time your data significantly changes. This will allow you, should your phone be stolen or taken hostage, to access your account and delete the phone while still having all your data.

Email and computers

Create a clean e mail address that you only use on your phone and set it up on your "clean phone." Use it occasionally and only give the address to highly trusted and reliable contacts. Ensure that your contact list on your phone has all of your contacts e mail addresses as well as their phone numbers in the address book. With your known email accounts you have to assume that they are "compromised or cloned" as a matter of course. To that end keep your e mail traffic flowing but slowly reduce the importance of the content making the content of less use to him over time. Make no drastic or noticeable changes.

Erase your search history as a matter of routine and if questioned say that you have been advised through business contacts to always delete your history and it lowers your exposure to DDOS (Distributed Denial of Service), Phishing and Ransomware attacks. Effectively, you are employing responsible IT procedures in order to protect the family business and its wealth.

Buy a tablet type computer and again synchronise it routinely with your cloud account including your email. Having your information in your cloud account gives you control of what you want to expose and allows you to protect it appropriately. Additionally, it reduces paperwork and the opportunity for you to be snooped on or called to account. You have to assume that when you do leave, all hardware, phones, computers and tablets could be seized, stolen or smashed.

Set up a DropBox account and save all work to it. Slowly reduce as much of your information that requires protection or is important and replace it with information that looks interesting but is in effect bland, useless and old news. Split financial correspondence into what is important and of use to him and what is not. This is difficult to do but it is worth spending time getting the balance right. Remember the key thing here is "staying grey". Do nothing to raise the fact that you are up to something. Do not rush, instead change things in small, hardly detectable increments. Patience and a bit of additional discomfort will pay off in the end. Slowly filter your important correspondence to your new e mail address that is totally divorced from your home computer or business laptop.

This new e mail, device and drop box is your new life going forward. Make the new e mail address totally disassociated from you so no maiden names, kids names, references to work or hobbies, interests and memorable dates. happy@thegreatescape.com might not work.

Running away money

If your salary or earnings go into a joint bank account there's nothing you can do to hide it from a coercively controlling partner. Even if you do have a sole account and your partner was aware of that, your options are limited. For instance, if your employer pays all of your salary into that account, if you start siphoning some of this off into a secret account it is easily spottable and identifiable, especially if you have online banking and a coercive partner as they inevitably will, access this to check on you. There could be serious repercussions for you if they discovered this siphoning off. The safest way to siphon money out of your account would be to first of all not have online banking. This makes everything much more visible. Physical statements are also visible but less immediate. Secondly, whether you have online banking or not, you will not need to build your running away stash slowly, carefully and invisibly. This is best done by withdrawing modest amounts of physical cash that do not attract suspicion and then redeposit this cash in a separate account of which your partner knows nothing.

Dostoevsky called money "coined liberty." Today we would need coins of gold to finance the cost of liberty and they are a good part of the plan. But banknotes are easier to hide. Think of them as "printed liberty."

Have you seen the film *Sleeping with the Enemy*, starring Julia Roberts and Kevin Kline? If you have, you know what I mean when I say you need to keep a grab bag ready for that moment when you need to escape (if and when you do flee, do not throw your wedding ring down the loo).

The grab bag needs to contain cash and over the preceding months/years, you need to have to have prepared the ground with physical and electronics secrets – as above.

The safe house and escape plan

This can be a difficult one as you really have to stay away from the usual suspects who could be placed under duress following your escape. The best option is that despite the love and trust of friends or relatives it is safer to have to rely on no one at all other than yourself until such times as the dust has settled and you have weighed up the impact of your actions. A safe place to keep your escape pack is also a challenge as the result of the pack being compromised could be significant, especially if it is an abusive relationship. A locker in a secured area is an option, some gyms have them that you can rent. Use a gym that you only go to occasionally and that he knows nothing about. The cover should it be discovered, could be a new class that you're going to with your female friends. Change the locker frequently. Lockers at work can also be an option along with rail stations etc where they are appropriately secured and covered by CCTV. Check them frequently and change them often. A safety deposit box is also an option if you can open an account with a different bank to the family bank. Make sure that it is a paperless service and all communication goes to your "dark" email account. Start to filter an amount away from all withdrawals that you make and secure that in your escape pack but again don't go overboard. Consider "losing" valuable jewellery and "finding" it in your safety box or somewhere else as a backup rather than gold coins. If you can, buy expensive stuff that is resalable should the need occur or keep-able if not.

The more financially literate you are, the easier it will be to amass your running away money.

To sum up

We are secretive about money, sometimes for good reasons, sometimes not. Controlling someone's money or their ability to make money is abuse. Plain and simple.

For generations women have been limited in our independent earning capacity, by law, by education, by common practice. These patriarchal legacies live on, meaning economic and financial abuse are often easily hidden, making them hard to fight. But there *are* means of escape and there are emergency services ready to take your calls and places you can go. See Useful Resources at the end of the book.

This disproportionately affects women and goes in hand-in-hand with other forms of abuse such as sexual and violent abuse. The bitter irony is that the women most affected are rendered the least able to escape.

Either way, the damage lingers on in the form of coerced debt and reduced earnings long after the abuse itself might have finished.

What government can do:

- Set up more refuges
- Create publicity campaigns explaining that financial and economic abuse *are* abuse
- Publicise what sufferers can do to escape them and find support
- Recognise that early economic abuse can manifest in the school system
- Educate teachers and social services how to spot it and what to do about it
- Educate pupils, both boys and girls, about what it is so they can spot it, seek help or offer help

What companies can do:

- Be aware of situations where coerced debt could be forced upon someone
- Be aware of situations when assets are annexed under coercion
- Employees need to be trained to spot this and report suspicions when they see it
- Human Resources departments can also look out for apparent curtailment of employees' economic and professional agency and offer them support

What you can do:

- Recognise that this is abuse

- Seek help
- If in imminent danger, get the hell out
- If you do you have the luxury of time, start planning very carefully
- The more financially literate you are, the easier this will be
- Amass your running away money in whichever way you can

Chapter Twelve

The gender wealth gap

- It could take another two centuries to close the gender financial wealth gap as men continue to control the majority of the world's financial assets
- In the United States, the gender wealth gap is much bigger than the gender wage gap. Families headed by women have just 55 cents in median wealth for every dollar of wealth owned by families headed by men
- Relative to the median wealth per every dollar held by families headed by non-Hispanic white men:
  - Non-Hispanic white women own 56 cents
  - Hispanic women own 10 cents
  - Non-Hispanic black women own 5 cents
- In the UK, women hold just £14.3 billion in investments to the £29.3 billion held by men
- Elsewhere in Europe, there are gaps in gross wealth of 27% in Slovakia, 33% in France, 44% in Austria, 45% in Germany, and 48% in Greece

All of the gaps I have discussed above -

- The pay gap
- The pension gap
- The care gap
- The motherhood penalty
- The opportunity gap
- The aspiration gap
- The debt gap
- The access to capital gap
- The mortgage gap
- The language gap
- the investment gap
- The money psychology gap

And the greater incidence of women suffering from financial abuse, all come together to create the most stubborn and consequential gap of them all: *the wealth gap.*

What is the gender wealth gap?

The gender wealth gap measures the difference between the average net worth of men and women - the assets they own minus the debts they carry.

Wealth inequality is greater than income inequality but unfortunately, despite its importance, much less is known about it. This is partly due to the comparative lack of data on wealth compared to data on income and also the challenges of deciphering who owns what within households.

But wealth data is arguably the most important metric to observe when analysing the position of women in society. It represents current inequalities, the legacy of past inequalities and it in turn drives future inequalities. This makes it more stubborn and enduring than income gaps, and more consequential: it influences just about everything: our overall economic prosperity, our health and well-being, our security both today and tomorrow. Wealth can provide a buffer against the interruption of income due to economic events or ill health. Wealth can give us resilience, flexibility, choices, freedom, safety. As well as economic power, it creates and denotes social and political power.

The big picture is it could take another two centuries to close the gender financial wealth gap as men continue to control the majority of the world's financial assets.[265]

So let's start with the big picture and some caveats. Reports are often compiled using different kinds of averaging (mean versus median) which throw up different results though the overall conclusions remain the same - sizeable gender wealth gaps exist. Secondly, I need to emphasise that this averaging masks huge inequalities that become stark and shocking when we narrow our focus.

Research from the Boston Consulting Group[266] shows average wealth by gender in different regions of the world as follows.

- Women in North America hold 37% of the North American wealth pie
- Women in Australia, New Zealand, and the Pacific Islands hold 33% of their regional pie
- Women in Asia (excluding Japan) hold 32%
- Western European women hold 31%
- Latin American women hold 25.5%
- Eastern European women (including Russia) hold 22.4%
- Middle Eastern and African women hold 20.4%
- Japanese women hold 16.6% of the Japanese pie

When we move away from the overall averages and take a closer look at wealth gaps by ethnicity, the figures become truly shocking.

Gender and ethnicity wealth gaps in the United States

The gender wealth gap is much bigger than the gender wage gap. Families headed by women have just 55 cents in median wealth for every dollar of wealth owned by families headed by men.[267]

If we disaggregate the figures by race, the numbers become so shocking I find them hard to process. Using results from the 2019 Federal Reserve Board's Survey of Consumer Finances, researchers point to the following enormous gaps.

Relative to the median wealth per every dollar held by families headed by non-Hispanic white men:

- Non-Hispanic white women own 56 cents
- Hispanic men own 22 cents
- Non-Hispanic black men own 19 cents
- Hispanic women own 10 cents
- Non-Hispanic black women own 5 cents

This is the legacy of centuries of inequality; generations of prejudice; of barriers; of health and educational provision, in short, of unequal opportunities which perpetuate unequal outcomes.

The picture in the UK

Obtaining data on wealth segregated by gender in the United Kingdom is almost impossible to come by. One proxy is financial investments where there is a £15 billion gender investment gap. Women hold just £14.3 billion in investments to the £29.3 billion held by men.

As Thomas Piketty pointed out in *Capital*, the fastest route to wealth creation and the most secure means of wealth preservation is not by selling our labour: it is by having access to capital, by having financial assets or real assets that work 24/7. We have seen the gaps in income and pensions. One way to sidestep this, to help build and sustain our financial future, to more fully participate in the economy, in the money world, is to go our own way via entrepreneurship rather than selling our labour. Is via starting and growing our own businesses.

This of course will depend on our access to capital which as we have seen is severely curtailed despite the fact when we do receive venture capital funding, we tend to out-perform male only ventures.

But figures for overall wealth by gender... Where are they??

There is wealth data compiled by the Office for National Statistics which is segregated by race but not by gender within the different racial groups. This data reveals the existence of large racial wealth gaps as we shall see below. It is reasonable to assume that given the prevalence of the gender gaps covered in this book, women in these different racial categories will come off worse than men.

A study published by the Resolution Foundation in December 2020[268] reported that people of black African ethnicity typically hold the lowest wealth - a median figure of £24,000 family wealth per adult, compared to £31,000 for Bangladeshi families, £41,800 for mixed white and black Caribbean ethnicity and £197,000 for those of white British ethnicity. The report finds that relative wealth gaps have fallen slightly over the decade from 2006-08 to 2016-18. The disparity between the lowest- and highest-wealth ethnic groups is down from 81 to 76 per cent of the highest-wealth group's average wealth.

The report lays bare the precariousness of families on the eve of the pandemic, with at least half Black African, Bangladeshi and Black Caribbean ethnicity households in the UK having less than £1,000 in family savings to act as an emergency buffer in case of a fall in their income or unexpected expenses.

The legacy effect of wealth created or not created by previous generations is revealed in inheritance which perpetuates these wealth gaps. The average person of white British ethnicity inherited a total of £3,068 from friends and family. Individuals from the next highest-inheriting ethnic group, people of Indian ethnicity, inherited on average £1,958, while those of black Caribbean ethnicity inherited £778. Those of black African, Chinese, Bangladeshi or Pakistani ethnicity typically inherited nothing.

The picture in Europe

Wealth data segregated by race in Europe is hard to come by. Information is more readily available by gender, although there is still a paucity. One report analysing the gap between male and female single households using 2010 household finance and consumption data for eight European countries[269] reveals a gap in gross wealth of 27% in Slovakia, 33% in France, 44% in Austria, 45% in Germany, and 48% in Greece.

A report[270] published by the London School of Economics, *Investigating the Gender Wealth Gap across Occupational Classes* in Germany, raises another potential cause of the wealth gap beyond the well established determinants.

The Precariat

They argue that women cluster in occupations that "systematically restrict them from wealth accumulation - precarious, low prestige and low-income occupations with high shares of part-time employment."

The authors go on to state that: "women's lower levels of wealth are further the result of the systematic devaluation of female occupations... Though women are oftentimes key workers – as currently exemplified in the COVID-19 pandemic – the systematic devaluation and lack of power resources restrict women from keeping up with male levels of income and wealth."

Power resources such as job security, unionization or the presence of strong lobby groups either enable or restrict women when it comes to saving and making long term-investment decisions like buying a home or investing in the stock market, which as we've seen above are both key components of wealth creation and protection.

It makes sense that if your job is precarious, you are less likely to make long-term investments as you need to keep a higher cash buffer on hand in the event of job loss or income interruptions.

This raises important questions such as: what do we value as a society? What occupations do we depend on? What should we reward more generously? Such perception-based phenomena are not surprising in a world where economics is a profession dominated by men, where the nature of the economy itself, and the prevailing economic philosophies, have been crafted over centuries by men, and, arguably, for men.

Men dominate the economics profession

In the US only 13% of academic economists are female and in the UK only 15%[271]. In Europe's top 20 economics schools only 12% of professors are female. One of only two women to win the Nobel Prize in economics, Esther Duflo, notes that the profession "is not intentionally sexist, but it's become sexist because the broader social environment is such that women are trained to be polite, and not to interrupt, and to let people finish their sentences ...in an environment where it's fair game to interrupt people and not let them finish their thought, it's more or conducive to men and also women just honestly don't like it." [272]

Others are not so sanguine about the profession. In 2018, the American Economic Association described the profession as hostile and discriminatory, including reports of bullying, bigotry, sexism and racism, and formulated a code of conduct In an attempt to rectify this.

Burn it down: economics failed us

That is the view of former U.S. Federal Reserve economist Claudia Sahm, who notes in a blog[273] that excoriates her profession: "Economics is a disgrace. The lack of diversity and inclusion degrades our knowledge and policy advice. We hurt economists from undergraduate classrooms to offices at the White House. We drive away talent; we mistreat those who stay; and we tolerate bad behaviour." She goes on to say that the toxic culture of economics reduces the quality of our economic policy advice, citing numerous examples of what she calls the elites circling the wagons to protect the prevailing theories and policies that they have promulgated from challenge by those of other demographics whether they be racial or gender.

The problem at the moment is that the more senior the position, the less diverse is the pool of economists from which to pick. Those seeking to employ a higher percentage of female economists note the lack of female economics graduates from which to choose.

Looking at my own experience of economics, as the daughter, and sister of two male, economics professors, and having studied it at Oxford, I've seen the lack of women directly. The ratio of students studying Politics, Philosophy and Economics at my Oxford College was 6:1 male:female. Looking at the data for 2020, the figures have improved. 37% of the total Oxford intake as a whole for PPE was female, which contrasts with 63% for medicine; 56% biochemistry; 62% biology; 77% biomedical sciences; 72% English; 30% Economics and Management; 30% maths.

Why, when women are increasingly entering hitherto male professions such as medicine and sciences, are we still shying away from economics and maths? It would seem likely that the culture around these subjects at schools (if economics is taught at all at certain schools) might be to blame. Women and girls might perceive that these are not subjects suitable for them. Much has been written about gender stereotypes which suggest that girls are not good at maths which will undoubtedly have put off many girls who would have been good at maths if they had only been given the opportunity and belief in their potential themselves and been encouraged to by a more supportive culture. It's likely that the same perception is dissuading girls from choosing to study economics. Given that economics is the closest any of us get to studying money at school or university this is proof again that women are being ruled out or are choosing to rule ourselves out of active participation in the money world to a much greater extent than men.

It will be interesting to see what percentage of the 2020 Oxford PPE intake continue in the profession and rise to positions of power whether in academia or in policy-enacting (and arguably making) institutions such as the Bank of England.

What is certain is that the economy in which we live has been molded by men. The old paradigm of annual GDP growth being the guiding force to which we must all bow our backs, regardless of the costs to us and to the planet, must be replaced. What is deemed valuable and what is not even measured in official figures, needs to be re-calibrated. Care-giving does not compute, in terms of what it contributes both practically and economically or in terms of what it costs the caregiver in terms of lost income, lost opportunities, lower wealth. That needs to change.

What emerges here is that the consequences of the dominance of the economics profession by men adversely affects not just the economics profession itself but the societies in which we live and our quality of life.

To sum up:

When we look at wealth gaps by gender and by ethnicity and gender, the picture is truly shocking. We see in these gaps the manifestation of the underlying array of gaps, biases, obstacles, prejudices, legacies and controls that still hold us back, and make us poorer than men.

We see the results of *generations* of these other gaps. We see the true scale of the problem and the magnitude of the action that needs to be taken.

Facile arguments such as women *choose* not to work in certain high-paying occupations, or women *choose* to work shorter hours or give up outside work altogether once they've had children, that girls *choose* not to study economics and maths infuriate me because they beg the question, *why are girls and women making these choices?* Are they really choices or are they born of necessity, biases, conscious and unconscious? And are they born out of outdated patriarchal work practices and ethoses that make certain occupations deeply toxic for women and unhealthy for all?

If the pay gap means that women are paid less than men, then women are guided by economic exigencies to be the one who cuts back her hours, who even gives up her job rather than her male partner. Even if this is meant to be a temporary workplace interruption it will affect her current and her long-term financial health - her National Insurance contributions and workplace pension contributions will be suspended, her earnings prospects dented even if she does return to work as a consequence of missing out on promotions and pay increases that go with them or pay rises that simply accrue with uninterrupted years of service.

If the social expectations means that it's more appropriate for the woman to stay at home with the children than it is for men, if the social expectation remains that men who take their paternity leave can't be that serious about their work or are somehow unmanly, unbreadwinnery, then the choices made do not reflect open and free ones but are instead made on the basis of prejudice

If girls are raised to believe that they are not good at maths and economics is not for them then it's no wonder they make choices to avoid those subjects.

These *choices* lead to a compounding effect of consequences that have enormous impacts on women's wealth and long-term financial health and abundance.

What needs to be done:

In the same way that you cannot pursue happiness directly but instead need to travel the roads that lead to it, you can't solve the wealth gap directly. You need to address the issues I've raised in the preceding chapters.

But one thing governments can do directly is obtain more statistics to show where the gaps manifest, which will help inform what needs to be done.

Conclusion

Government, companies and all of us as individuals need to work to boost individual financial literacy from a young age up. As ever, education is our friend.

We've seen how increased financial literacy, how casting light on our own psychologies and those around us, and how unearthing biases both conscious and unconscious, can help fight the various gaps.

Like happiness, the roads to solve the wealth gap involve tangible and intangibles.

The tangibles are to remove structural inequalities, to make childcare more affordable, to increase equality of opportunity, to foster greater diversity.

This will pay dividends in many areas.

The patriarchy is leaving money on the table and that they don't like.

We've seen that boards with more women on them increase that company's profitability.

We've seen that female-lead venture capital prospects out-perform the male-lead ones.

Diversity is profitable apart from being the right course of action to follow on the road for greater social equity. It creates inspiring role models, helps break stereotypes and in so doing creates a virtuous circle.

It helps to tackle the intangibles which lie behind the wealth gap: the way we think, the way others think, the conscious and unconscious biases we hold.

The money world needs to become much more diverse and inclusive; to speak to women in a way that engages us, serves our distinct, multiple, and changing requirements, and aligns with our values.

It needs to recruit more women. A greater deploying of the female gaze will in turn change the way the money world speaks to us and encourage more women to follow in the footsteps of these role models.

As well as deploying the female gaze and bringing extra profitability to companies, we can also deploy our own characteristics to make more money for ourselves.

We have a superpower, I call it the Alchemy of Humility. In the same way that men hate asking for directions even if lost, they tend to over-back themselves when it comes to picking stock market investments whereas we are more likely to either ask and to be conscious of the possibility of mis-steps. This shows up in our relative shunning of single company bets, (men are more likely to attempt to back individual winners) and our preference to diversify our options and back a range of companies in a fund. Also, we are less prone to 'investing thrill-seeking.' This means we trade less, and as a result suffer less drag on our returns from the costs of trading. We do not try and be clever-clever and time the market.

We are more humble and it pays.

This humility might be inherited, it might be as a result of the patriarchy having knocked our confidence and sense of agency but, either way, we can turn it around and make it work for us. And that at least offers us a silver lining.

Looking at the bigger picture, we need to make the economics profession more appealing to girls and women.

We need more female economists.

We need new economic models, philosophies and policies.

I don't want to *lean in* any more. I admire Sheryl Sandberg enormously but I don't want to elevate work to a godlike status. There has to be balance. I don't want to step into that whole patriarchal mindset. When I first went into the City, I had to lean in. I leant in so far I'm amazed I was still standing after eight years. People would talk with awe and warped respect about two of the leading firms, one in investment banking, one in management consultancy, who boasted the top divorce rates. This was meant to be a good thing! This was meant to and did attract people to work there in a masochistic urge to see how much they could take and just how far they were willing to go to prove themselves truly 'committed.' This is the value system that has been promulgated. This is the value system that still (hopefully to a slightly lesser extent) operates in certain spheres. Is it any wonder that many women are unable or chose not to walk into that world because of our care responsibilities?

These toxic work practices and work- place values need to change.

Old paradigms of GDP growth being the be all and end all need to change.

This obsession with GDP growth not only impoverishes our own resources but impoverishes the planet because its predicated on constantly extracting more resources from the earth, and constantly making us buy things, and perpetuating this consumer society where we are never sated, where needs are constantly being created and a dynamic has been forged where only the perpetual act of purchasing helps to stave off existential feelings, existential fears of what it's all about, of why am I doing this and why am I working here and what is the payback?

The payback is buying more and more stuff and having less and less space to store it in as houses get more and more expensive, as we can afford only smaller and smaller homes and we have to subcontract our stuff out to other homes – storage facilities.

There are so many different threads here. Spending slow, freeing up time, stuff versus time.

We're drowning in stuff, the planet is drowning in stuff, meanwhile the planet has been impoverished as resources are ripped out of it beyond its ability to renew them. This economic/consumption model doesn't serve us, it doesn't serve the planet, it serves some very rich and ever richening individuals and companies who exploit our scarcity complexes.

I'm not knocking capitalism per se. I'm searching for a better version.

We need to redefine what gross domestic product actually is. We need to look at what we value as individuals and as a society, all the unpaid hours of care that don't factor into or increase gross domestic product but involve considerable sacrifices on our part and on the part of carers of whatever gender.

These economic models were created in a world of less scarcity, of lower population, of more plentiful resources in comparison with the demand for them but we have gone beyond that point and we need new economic models to reflect this new reality. These old models do not serve us anymore.

We are like hamsters on a wheel, running and running and running and getting nowhere.

John Elkington, one of the pioneers of sustainable economics, brought into the consciousness the concepts of

People, Profit, Planet as guiding lights.

To that I would add my own tilt:

Finance, feminism, freedom.

Money is a feminist issue and that makes it an issue for all humankind.

Acknowledgements

I want to thank my husband, Rupert Wise, whose love and support in every possible way means so much to me and makes so much possible. He also happens to have a fair degree of expertise on this subject.

My brothers, Roy Davies and Ken Davies, have read and annotated the manuscript with very helpful corrections and suggestions and Roy in particular has dedicated a great deal of time to checking my multiple sources and references. Huge thanks to you, brothers.

I want to remember and thank those presences in my mind and my heart, my late father, Professor Glyn Davies and my late brother Professor Dr John Eric Davies, economists both, my father's specialty being money and the history of money. I hear their wise voices in my head as I write. I'm sure they would have had much to say and much help to give but I hope I have done them proud.

Useful resources

Multiple aspects of the Money World:

Money Saving Expert

Money-savingexpert.com is an invaluable resource across multiple aspects of the financial world including bank accounts, pensions and investing, mortgages, income and budgeting, students' financial issues, credit cards and loans, credit scores and debt help and more.

Debt

Step Change

Step Change are a UK charity and have a free debt advice service. In 2022 they helped 25,516 clients become debt free .

https://www.stepchange.org/

Debtors Anonymous (DA)

Debtors Anonymous (DA) is a twelve-step programme for anyone who wants to stop incurring unsecured debt.

DA encourages careful record keeping and monitoring of finances – including purchases, income, and debt payments – so that you get a clearer picture of your spending habits. This information is used to develop healthier spending practices, supporting you in keeping a reasonable quality of life while still repaying debt. Similarly, DA recommends developing plans for the future to increase your income.

Fair4All Finance

Fair4allfinance.org.uk They note: "Millions of people are unable to access mainstream products and services others rely on to meet their financial needs. Without safety nets like credit, insurance or savings, everyday life events or financial shocks can tip people into vulnerable circumstances."

They go on to say "Our programmes increase access to fair and affordable financial products and services in some of the most deprived areas of the country:"

N.B. The organisation has a Resources Page which includes a list of FAQ which is quite interesting, particularly the last question "What about APR?" which discusses the limitations of the Annual Percentage Rate when it comes to judging the fairness of lending agreements.

Illegal Money Lending Team

A department of the UK government. You can report loan sharks online anonymously.

England, Wales, Scotland and Northern Ireland have different phone numbers, websites and email addresses so check them independently.

Financial advisors:

Vouchedfor

VouchedFor.co.uk has a comprehensive list by region which names their top rated financial advisors and the firms they work for. These advisors are fully verified members of Vouchedfor which means that Vouchedfor has checked with the FCA/and/or the firm's senior managers that they have the necessary permissions to practice.

Pensions

You can find out more on the following government website but there are also other sources of information available in useful resources at the end of the book.

Retirement Planning
https://www.yourpension.gov.uk

UK Pension Advice Service
https://www.nationalpensionadvisors.co.uk/official

The Money and Pensions Service
Building financial well-being

https://moneyandpensionsservice.org.uk

Pensions - Citizens Advice

https://www.citizensadvice.org.uk › debt-and-money

Pension Bee led by Romi Savova

Many people have a number of different pension pots. PensionBee is an organisation for people wanting to combine and transfer their old pensions into a brand new online plan.

PensionBee was founded by Romi Savova in 2014 after the problems she encountered in transferring her own pensions. https://www.pensionbee.com

Planning and preparing for retirement age UK

https://www.ageuk.org.uk › work-learning › retirement

And, crucially, beware fraudsters.

How to spot a pension scam

https://www.moneyhelper.org.uk/en/money-troubles/scams/how-to-spot-a-pension-scam

It would be advisable to read this BEFORE making any major decisions.

Mental health

Mind

Mental health Information and support

Mind helps people experiencing a mental health problem. They offer:

- An Infoline, which offers callers confidential help for the price of a local call.
- A Legal Line, which provides information on mental health related law to the public, service users, family members/carers, mental health professionals and mental health advocates.
- And award-winning information

https://www.mind.org.uk/about-us/what-we-do/

Venture Capital

The British Business Bank

The British Business Bank is owned by the government. It is its economic development bank whose self-avowed purpose is to make financial markets work better for small businesses.

Domestic violence and abuse - getting help

This advice applies to England.

Organisations for women

National Domestic Abuse helpline

freephone 24 hour helpline which provides advice and support to women and can refer them to emergency accommodation.

Website: www.nationaldahelpline.org.uk

Refuge

Refuge provides safe, emergency accommodation through a network of refuges throughout the UK, including culturally-specific services for women from minority ethnic communities and cultures.

Their website also includes some information for men who are either being abused or who are abusers.

Website: www.refuge.org.uk

Women's Aid

The Women's Aid website provides a wide range of resources to help women and young people.

This includes The Survivor's Handbook which provides a range of information including legal and housing advice, tips on how to create a safety plan and advice for people with specialist housing needs. It's available in 11 languages and in audio.

They also run a website to support to children and teenagers who may be living in a home affected by domestic violence, or who may be in a violent relationship themselves.

Website: www.womensaid.org.uk

Rights of Women

Rights of Women offers confidential legal advice on domestic and sexual violence. Website: www.rightsofwomen.org.uk

Finding Legal Options for Women Survivors (FLOWS)

FLOWS gives legal advice to women who are affected by domestic abuse - they also give advice to front line workers.

Website: www.rcjadvice.org.uk/family/flows-finding-legal-options-for-women-survivors

Southall Black Sisters

Southall Black Sisters provide advice for Black (Asian and African-Caribbean) women with issues including domestic abuse, forced marriage, immigration and homelessness.

Website: www.southallblacksisters.org.uk

Organisations for women and men

RCJ Advice Family Service

RCJ Advice Family Service can give legal advice to people who are affected by domestic abuse or need family law help – find out more on the RCJ Advice website.

Rape Crisis

Rape Crisis (England and Wales) is an umbrella organisation for Rape Crisis Centres across England and Wales. The website has contact details for centres and gives basic information about rape and sexual violence for survivors, friends, family, students and professionals. Rape Crisis (England and Wales) also runs a freephone helpline.

Website: www.rapecrisis.org.uk

Honour Network Helpline

The Honour Network Helpline is a national helpline run by Karma Nirvana, a national charity which advises victims and survivors of forced marriage and honour-based abuse.

Website: www.karmanirvana.org.uk

Hourglass

Hourglass gives confidential advice and information to older people who are victims of violence or abuse. A relative or friend of the person being abused can also contact the helpline on behalf of the older person. The helpline can be used in the case of older people who live at home, in a care home or who are in hospital.

Website: wearehourglass.org

National Stalking Helpline

The National Stalking Helpline can provide advice on how to deal with any type of stalking behaviour. This includes advice on how to report the behaviour to the police, and what you can expect if you report something.

Website: www.stalkinghelpline.org

Respect Phoneline

Respect Phoneline offers information and advice to partners, friends and family who want to stop someone's violent behaviour.

Website: www.respectphoneline.org.uk

Safelives

Safelives helps more than 65,000 adults and 85,000 children each year.

www.safelives.org.uk

Wiltshire Bobby Van Trust

WBVT works in partnership with the local police to help the over-sixties, the disabled and victims of domestic abuse to feel safer at home.

www.wiltshirebobbyvan.org.uk

Organisations for lesbian, gay, bisexual and transgender people

National LGBT+ Domestic Abuse Helpline

Galop provides support for lesbian, gay, bisexual and transgender people experiencing domestic violence.

Website: www.galop.org.uk/get-help

Organisations for disabled people

SignHealth - Domestic Abuse Service

SignHealth provides a specialist domestic abuse service to help Deaf people find safety and security. You can find out how to contact them on their website.

Website: www.signhealth.org.uk/with-deaf-people/domestic-abuse/domestic-abuse-service/

Respond

Respond work with children and adults with learning disabilities who've either experienced abuse or abused other people.

Website: www.respond.org.uk

Bibliography

All the books referenced in my earlier book, *10 Things Everyone Needs to Know About Money;* and...

Invisible Women: Exposing Data Bias in A World Designed For Men, Caroline Criado Perez, Vintage Books, 2020

Career & Family: Women's Century-Long Journey Toward Equity, Claudia Goldin, Princeton University Press, 2021

A Room of One's Own and *Three Guineas,* Virginia Woolf, William Collins, 2014

Payback: Debt and The Shadow Side of Wealth, Margaret Atwood, Bloomsbury, 2008

Capital In the Twenty-First Century, Thomas Piketty, Harvard University Press, 2017

The Gendered Brain: The New Neuroscience That Shatters the Myth Of The Female Brain, Gina Rippon, Vintage, 2020

Testosterone: Sex, Power, and The Will to Win by Joe Herbert, Oxford University Press, 2015

Testosterone Rex: Unmaking the Myths Of Our Gendered Minds, Cordelia Fine, Icon Books, 2017

Having And Being Had, Eula Biss, Faber & Faber, 2021

Money: The Unauthorised Biography, Felix Martin, Vintage Books, 2014

Double Lives: A History of Working Motherhood, Helen McCarthy, Bloomsbury, 2021

The National Debt: A Short History, Martin Slater, Hurst & Company, 2018

Sex, Money, Happiness and Death: The Quest For Authenticity, Manfred

F.R. Kets de Vries, Palgrave Macmillan, 2016

Difficult Women: A History of Feminism In 11 Fights, Helen Lewis, Jonathan Cape, 2020

The Authority Gap: Why Women Are Still Taken Less Seriously Than Men, And What We Can Do About It, Mary Ann Sieghart, Black Swan, 2022

Mind Over Money: The Psychology of Money and How To Use It Better, Claudia Hammond, Canongate Books, 2016

The Psychology of Money: Timeless Lessons on Wealth, Greed, And Happiness, Morgan Housel, Harriman House, 2020

Why She Buys: The New Strategy for Reaching the World's Most Powerful Consumers, Bridget Brennan, Crown Business, 2011

Any book by Michael Lewis

Why Women Are Poorer Than Men and What We Can Do About It, Annabelle Williams, Penguin, 2020

Creditocracy: And the Case for Debt Refusal, Andrew Ross, OR Books, 2013

The High Price of Materialism, Tim Kasser, MIT Press, 2003

Hood Feminism: Notes from The Women White Feminists Forgot, Mikki Kendall, Bloomsbury, 2020

Loved Clothes Last, Orsola de Castro, Penguin, 2021

Understanding Consumer Financial Behaviour: Money Management in An Age Of Financial Illiteracy, W. Fred van Raaij, Palgrave Macmillan, 2016

Your Money or Your Life, Vicki Robin and Joe Dominguez, Penguin, 2008

Can't Even: How Millennials Became the Burnout Generation, Anne Helen Petersen, Chatto & Windus, 2021

Super Crunchers: How Anything Can Be Predicted, Ian Ayres, John Murray, 2007

The Oxford Handbook of The Sociology of Finance, edited by Karin Knorr Cetina and Alex Preda, Oxford University Press, 2012

Money: The True Story of a Made-Up Thing, Jacob Goldstein, Atlantic Books, 2020

Manias, Panics, And Crashes: A History of Financial Crises, 8th ed by Robert Z. Aliber, Charles P. Kindleberger and Robert N. McCauley, Palgrave Macmillan, 2023

The New Psychology of Money, Adrian Furnham, Routledge, 2014

Women's Rights: A Practical Guide, Anna Coote and Tess Gill, Penguin, 1981

Ladies of the Ticker: Women and Wall Street From The Gilded Age To The Great Depression, George Robb, University of Illinois Press, 2017

The Economic Psychology of Everyday Life, Paul Webley [et al.], Psychology Press, 2001

The Black Swan: The Impact of The Highly Improbable, Nassim Nicholas Taleb, Allen Lane, 2011 (and any other book by the same author)

Sheconomics: Add Power to Your Purse with The Ultimate Money Makeover, Karen J. Pine and Simonne Gnessen, Headline, 2009

A History of Money (4th ed) by Glyn Davies and Duncan Connors, University of Wales Press, 2016

Frozen Desire: An Inquiry into the Meaning of Money, James Buchan, Picador, 1997

Thinking, fast and slow, Daniel Kahneman, Penguin, 2012

Risk, Uncertainty and Profit, Frank H Knight, Harper & Row, 1965

Mastering Bitcoin 2e: Programming the Open Blockchain, Andreas M. Antonopoulos, O'Reilly, 2017

Unmasking Financial Psychopaths: Inside the Minds of Investors in the Twenty-First Century, Deborah W. Gregory, Palgrave Macmillan, 2014

About the Author

Born in Scotland and raised in South Wales, Linda inhaled books as a child and dreamed of becoming a writer. But she was the daughter of an economist and a homemaker and raised to be practical. So she went into investment banking instead. One day, to her horror, she figured out a way to commit the perfect financial crime. Instead of doing it, she quit her job and wrote about it. Nest of Vipers went on to be published in over 30 territories, optioned multiple times and has sold over three million copies. Linda has gone on to publish 14 more books, variously for adults, young adults and children, which collectively have sold millions of copies and won various awards.

She has lived in Peru and the Middle East with her husband and 3 children. In 2005, in what could have been ripped from the pages of her own books she and her husband were kidnapped, interrogated and held prisoner in Iran. She went on to write about this experience and what she learned from it in her first work of non-fiction, *Kidnapped*.

Linda also writes for The Times, Sunday Times, Daily Telegraph, Independent and the Guardian newspapers and the National Theatre. She is a winner of the Philip Geddes Prize for journalism. In 2019, Linda became the Inaugural Writer in Residence at St Edmund Hall, University of Oxford.

What Every Woman Needs to Know for Financial Abundance is the follow-on and companion to her earlier book, *10 Things Everyone Needs to Know About Money*.

Linda regularly appears at literary festivals, universities and schools and gives talks, workshops and master classes on how to develop and maintain a healthy relationship with money, and how to create both inner and outer abundance.

Linda is a fully qualified and certified Jungian life coach and specialises in coaching women on this subject. To find out more about her coaching, events and books please see www.lindadavies.com

Linda lives with her family, three rescue cats and two Rhodesian Ridgebacks near the sea in Suffolk. She is an avid sea swimmer and cold water aficionado.

Footnotes

[1] *Global Gender Gap Report 2020*, World Economic Forum, 2019

[2] *Cocoa Farmer Income: Report by True Price*, commissioned by Fairtrade International, 2018

[3] *The Invisible Women Behind Our Chocolate*, Fairtrade Foundation, 2020

[4] *Global Gender Gap Report 2020*, World Economic Forum, 2019

[5] *How to close the gender pay gap*, *Financial Times*, 6 August 2020

[6] *Gender pay gap in the UK: 2021*, Office for National Statistics, 2021

[7] National Women's Law Centre, 2020 report

[8] National Women's Law Center's (NWLC) analysis of U.S. Census data https://www.shrm.org/resourcesandtools/hr-topics/compensation/pages/wage-gap-is-wider-for-working-mothers.aspx. Mothers in the U.S. who work full time are paid an average of 69 cents for every $1 a father makes, or $18,000 less annually, according to the National Women's Law Center's (NWLC) analysis of U.S. Census data. The financial loss mothers experience is greater in some states and for women of colour who are mothers. In Louisiana and Utah, for example, mothers who work full time are paid 59 cents and 61 cents, respectively, for every dollar fathers make. Latina mothers are paid just 46 cents for every dollar paid to white, non-Hispanic fathers.

[9] Before and After: Gender Transitions, Human Capital, and Workplace Experiences https://www.degruyter.com/document/doi/10.2202/1935-1682.1862/html

[10] Erickson, Amy Louise, *Women and Property: In Early Modern England*, Routledge, 1995

[11] Global Gender Gap Index 2016

[12] Gender Pay Gap in the UK: 2022, Office for National Statistics, 26 October 2022

[13] Breach, Anthony; Li, Yaojun. Gender Pay Gap by Ethnicity in Britain. London: Fawcett Society, 2017 https://www.research.manchester.ac.uk/portal/files/52919431/Breach_and_Li_2017_Gender_Pay_Gap_by_Ethnicity_in_Britain.pdf

[14] Source: as note 13 above

[15] 2022 State of the Gender Pay Gap Report by Payscale https://www.payscale.com/research-and-insights/gender-pay-gap/

[16] Goldin, Claudia Career and Family, Princeton University Press, 2021

[17] The Wage Gap: The Who, How, Why, and What to Do: Fact Sheet. National Women's Law Center, September 2021 https://www.pewresearch.org/

[18] As note 17 above

[19] https://www.aauw.org/resources/article/equal-pay-day-calendar/

[20] This date is based on U.S. Census figures showing that the average woman who works full time is paid on average just 83 percent of the typical man's pay

[21] https://www.fawcettsociety.org.uk/news/the-fawcett-society-announces-date-of-equal-pay-day-2021 Fawcett uses the mean, full-time, hourly gender pay gap for the UK to calculate the gender pay gap for Equal Pay Day which in 2021 is 11.9%, an increase from 10.6% in 2020

[22] *Amanda Serrano And Katie Taylor Will Earn Seven Figures for Their Fight, Say Jake Paul And Eddie Hearn, Forbes*, 4 February 2022 https://www.forbes.com/sites/brianroberts/2022/02/04/amanda-serrano-katie-taylor-to-earn-7-figures-per-eddie-hearn-jake-paul/

[23] *From Ian Wright to Dame Laura Kenny, stars back new Telegraph campaign to close gender prize-money gap, The Telegraph*, 24 March 2022

[24] The National Women's Law Center Report October 2020 https://nwlc.org/wp-content/uploads/2019/09/Wage-Gap-Who-how.pdf

[25] *Career and Family*, p.165

[26] Henrik Kleven, an economist at Princeton University, analysed data from Denmark, a country that offers new parents a whole year of paid childcare leave and also which subsidises heavily the cost of nursery care for children under 3.

[27] Harvard economist Claudia Goldin reports that the gender wage gap in America is the largest for women in their 30s — classic childbearing years

[28] The y axis in the original had units 0.1, 0.2 etc being factors of the "corrected" no children case (decimal points not clear on some versions of the paper). It might be clearer to label them -20%, -40% etc. The baseline is an estimated "no children" case. The graph shows that women with children take an immediate 30% hit relative to men, and never catch up again - with a long term gap of approx 20%.

[29] According to an analysis of Census data by the nonprofit advocacy organization National Women's Law Center in 2018

[30] OECD report Society at a Glance 2016

[31] Foster, Liam et al, *Closing the pension gap: Understanding women's attitudes to pension saving*, Fawcett Society, 2016. https://www.researchgate.net/publication/351878266_Understanding_Women%27s_Attitudes_to_Pension_Saving

[32] Noble, Johanna, *How to cut the costs of childcare: free nursery hours and tax-free childcare: who's eligible & how to claim, The Times Money Mentor*, updated 28 July 2022. https://www.thetimes.co.uk/money-mentor/article/cut-childcare-costs/

[33] Goldin, Claudia *Career and Family*, Princeton University Press, 2021

[34] *Women in the Workplace*, McKinsey & Company, 2022.

[35] *Hidden Figures*, a film directed by Theodore Melfi, 2016, is loosely based on the 2016 non-fiction book of the same name by Margot Lee Shetterly about African American female mathematicians who worked at NASA during the Space Race.

[36] *How to close the gender pay gap, Financial Times* 6 August 2020

[37] https://www.mckinsey.com/featured-insights/diversity-and-inclusion/women-in-the-workplace

[38] *Unpaid Care Work: The missing link in the analysis of gender gaps in labour outcomes*, OECD Development Centre, December 2014

[39] On sale in February 2022, emblazoned with messages

[40] Source: J. Britton, L. Dearden and B. Waltmann, 'The returns to undergraduate degrees by socio-economic group and ethnicity', Institute for Fiscal Studies, 2021, https://www.ifs.org.uk/publications/15383

[41] https://www.gohenry.com/uk/blog/news/why-is-there-a-pocket-money-pay-gap

[42] https://busykid.com/blog/gender-pay-gap-starts-with-kids-in-america/

[43] Dr David Whitebread and Dr Sue Bingham, *Habit formation and learning in young children* (May 2013). The study was commissioned by the Money Advice Service.

[44] On sale in February 2022, emblazoned with messages

[45] According to a report by the Higher Education Policy Institute - *Mind the (Graduate Gender Pay) Gap,* 12 November 2022, Bethan Cornell, Rachel Hewitt and Bahram Bekhradnia HEPI number 135

[46] Source: J. Britton, L. Dearden and B. Waltmann, 'The returns to undergraduate degrees by socio-economic group and ethnicity', Institute for Fiscal Studies, 2021, https://www.ifs.org.uk/publications/15383

[47] As per the range of sloganised clothes on sale in Primark in 2022 as quotes above and in *The Times* in February 2022.

[48] Source: J. Britton, L. Dearden and B. Waltmann, 'The returns to undergraduate degrees by socio-economic group and ethnicity', Institute for Fiscal Studies, 2021, https://www.ifs.org.uk/publications/15383

[49] *Religion, sex and politics? The M word is Britain's biggest taboo*, Lloyds Bank, 7 March 2019 https://www.lloydsbankinggroup.com/media/press-releases/2019/lloyds-bank/the-m-word-is-britains-biggest-taboo.html

[50] *Traditional fairy tales reimagined to tackle financial literacy gap between boys and girls*, HSBC UK News and Media, 2 October 2018 https://www.about.hsbc.co.uk/news-and-media/traditional-fairy-tales-reimagined-to-tackle-financial-literacy-gap-between-boys-and-girls

[51] https://www.independent.co.uk/news/uk/home-news/pay-rise-women-work-awkward-gender-pay-gap-a9147931.html

[52] Tali Mendelberg, professor of politics at Princeton, and Christopher Karpowitz, associate professor of political science at Brigham Young University in "The Silent Sex: Gender, Deliberation and Institutions"

[53] Carter et al, Women's disability in academic seminars

[54] Jacobi and schweers Justice, interrupted

[55] David Sadker and Myra Sadker's *Failing at Fairness: How America's Schools Cheat Girls,* published back in 1994, and *Still Failing at Fairness* published in 2009 cite their own research showing that at every grade level, teachers tend to pay more attention to boys in their classes, calling on them more often and asking them harder and more complicated questions than they do girls, particularly in maths and science.

[56] Parke, Fatherhood

[57] Esposito, *Sex differences in Children's Conversation*.

[58] *Why do so few men read books by women*? By MA Sieghart, *The Guardian*, 9 July 2021. https://www.theguardian.com/books/2021/jul/09/why-do-so-few-men-read-books-by-women Research from Nielsen Book research which shows that of the all time top 10 best selling female authors in the UK going back to Jane Austen, 19% of readers were men and 81% women, but of the all time top 10 best-selling books by male authors, 55% of readers were male and 45% female.

[59] Multiple studies across the world show this

[60] Data from the Fawcett Society report

[61] Scottish Widows Women & Retirement Press Release 2020 https://adviser.scottishwidows.co.uk/assets/literature/docs/2020-11-women-pension.pdf

[62] Another report published in 2019 using Department for Work and Pensions data analysed by the trade union Prospect revealed the gender pensions chasm in retirement earnings between men and women encompassing both their private and state pension was a staggering 40.3%

[63] https://group.legalandgeneral.com/en/newsroom/press-releases/legal-general-calls-for-urgent-action-as-uk-gender-pension-gap-makes-slow-progress

[64] The Scottish Widows study also suggested that the gender pensions gap widened during lockdown because more women were furloughed.

[65] IFS Briefing Note BN290, 2020

[66] COVID-19 Eroding Female Labor Force Participation and Growth, Citi Global Perspectives & Solutions (Citi GPS), 27 May 2020.

https://www.citivelocity.com/citigps/eroding-female-jobs/

[67] According to retirement research body the Pensions Policy Institute (PPI). https://www.pensionspolicyinstitute.org.uk/media/3679/20201208-the-underpensioned-index-report-final.pdf See also the detailed analysis of the data in the Index by NOW: Pensions. *The underpensioned report 2020: Examining the pension savings gaps for the most financially at-risk groups in our society*, NOW: Pensions, December 2020. Chapter 4:, Single mothers https://www.nowpensions.com/app/uploads/2022/10/NP266_Underpension_report_Feb2020.pdf However, on 21 March 2022 Now: Pensions issued a new report claiming that as a result of the Covid pandemic single mothers' pension pots had fallen by 40% from £18,300 to just £11,000 and 58% of single mothers are now ineligible for a workplace pension. *Single mothers' pension wealth is at an all-time low, dropping by 40% in the pandemic.* NOW: Pensions, 21 March 2022. https://www.nowpensions.com/press/single-mothers-pension-wealth-dropped-by-40-per-cent-in-pandemic/

[68] https://www.nowpensions.com/press/single-mothers-pension-wealth-dropped-by-40-per-cent-in-pandemic/

[69] https://www.familysearch.org/en/blog/100-years-ago-today-1920

[70] Understanding the Gender Pensions Gap, Pensions Policy Institute, 2019

---

[71] According to The Social Market Foundation in a 2021 report which notes "the demographic outlook suggests Britain could also face long-term shortages of working-age adults".

[72] According to data from the Office for National Statistics

[73] The ONS predicts that over the next 30 years childless women in their 80s will triple in Wales and England to 66,313.

[74] This can be done in various ways but I've simplified the net effect here for illustration purposes

[75] Ten years of Automatic Enrolment in Workplace Pensions: statistics and analysis, Department for Work and Pensions, 26 October 2022

[76] Resolution Foundation report

[77] The Fawcett Society Scottish Widows report of 2016 notes: "Many of the women described childcare as a cost paid from their incomes rather than as shared with their partners. This significantly limited their disposable income and ability to save for retirement."

[78] As quoted in https://darlingmagazine.co.uk/women-to-watch/women-in-business-science-tech/what-

[79] Data from the Fawcett Society report

[80] Scottish Widows, 2014

[81] Scottish Widows, 2015

[82] Standard Life study reveals major gaps in pension awareness, The Actuary, 18th October 2022 https://www.theactuary.com/news/2022/10/18/standard-life-study-reveals-major-gaps-pension-awareness

[83] *Will we ever summit the Pension Mountain? New analysis* from Royal London, 16 May 2018 https://www.royallondon.com/about-us/media/media-centre/press-releases/archive/skyrocketing-cost-of-retiring-for-young/

[84] In an article in the *Financial Times* Saturday, 12 September 2020 quoting the Police Foundation

[85] Skidmore, Michael, *Protecting people's pensions: understanding and preventing scams.* The Police Foundation, 2020

[86] FTSE 350 firms with more than 33% female membership on their executive committees have a net profit margin over 10 times greater than firms with no women in committee roles. As such, the UK economy has missed out on £47 billion of pre-tax profit. (*The Pipeline,* 27 July 2020)

[87] *Make money equal: linguistic analysis* Starling Bank, 2018

[88] Kanji, Shireen. *Summary report: gendered representations of money in visual media, a study.* Starling Bank, 2021

[89] According to a study by Equity Research firm Redburn and PWC in 2019

[90] As quoted in BBC News Magazine, 6 July 2016

[91] Credit card sexism: *The woman who couldn't buy a moped.* BBC News, 6 July 2016. https://www.bbc.co.uk/news/magazine-36662872

[92] This highlights a profound problem for women, where the inability to access a safe means of travelling to and from work (or anywhere for that matter) is an effective barrier to employment and to earning money on their own terms.

[93] According to a Mintel report *Women and Finance* and also discussed in an interesting Guardian article: *You've come a long way, Jenny* https://www.theguardian.com/money/2004/apr/18/womenandmoney.observercashsection

[94] In the FTSE 100, there are five female CEOs, and six CEOs named Peter

[95] According to a report on U.K. corporate leadership among 350 companies on the FTSE index by diversity and inclusion consultancy The Pipeline

[96] FTSE 350 firms with more than 33% female membership on their executive committees have a net profit margin over 10 times greater than firms with no women in committee roles. As such, the UK economy has missed out on £47 billion of pre-tax profit. (*The Pipeline,* 27 July 2020)

[97] According to research from comparison website Finder

[98] Looking at gender diversity in UK financial services

[99] As in other areas, women in larger companies fare better than the smaller ones, comprising 23% of the total compared to 17%

[100] According to a report in the *Harvard Business Review* by Paul Gompers and Silpa Kovvali

[101] Mean weekly gross earnings for male and female employees in the financial and insurance activities sector in the United Kingdom (UK) in 2022. Statista Research Department, Nov 14, 2022 https://www.statista.com/statistics/421874/mean-weekly-earnings-finance-insurance-both-genders/

[102] Women in Hedge Funds, Preqin, 2019 https://docs.preqin.com/reports/Preqin-Women-in-Hedge-Funds-February-2019.pdf

[103] UBS launches portfolio to invest in women-led hedge funds, Financial Times, 20 July 2021. An earlier Initiative by Aberdeen standard also targeted women-led hedge funds: Financial Times, 25 November 2020

[104] The Hedge Fund Review Women Access Index rose 6.5% while the general HFRI 500 weighted composite rose by 9.2%

[105] *Is gender diversity a game changer for investment decision makers?* UBS Asset Management, June 2021 https://www.ubs.com/uk/en/assetmanagement/insights/thematic-viewpoints/sustainable-impact-investing/articles/gender-diversity.html

[106] Women in finance annual review. HM Treasury, 2021. https://www.gov.uk/government/publications/new-financial-women-in-finance-annual-review-march-2021 https://www.womeninfinance.org.uk/d856e309-cbd1-4def-adde-553648611892

[107] *The fintech gender gap.* BIS Working Papers No 931 11 March 2021

[108] https://www.gu.se/en/about/find-staff/ylvabaeckstrom

[109] Quoted in *The Sunday Times*, March 27th 2022

---

[110] Inflation can conversely, also have a beneficial effect on debt in that it reduces the 'real' value of debt, which for those with rising incomes, can actually be an economic benefit - in 'real' terms, they repay less principal than they borrowed - but that's another argument. It's something I cover in detail in my earlier book *10 Things Everyone Needs to Know about Money,* Atebol, 2021

[111] Not to mention the cost of government and corporate debt which will impose huge new costs on both.

[112] https://www.thetimes.co.uk/article/women-charged-more-on-sexist-high-street-3gpwv2ck3qd

[113] A credit and financial management platform

[114] According to a survey of 1,012 UK adults carried out by Qualtrics Research between 16 February and 5 March 2021.

[115] https://www.fca.org.uk/publication/corporate/woolard-review-report.pdf

[116] Household debt and gender: pre-budget briefing from the Women's Budget Group March 2020 https://wbg.org.uk/wp-content/uploads/2020/02/final-debt-2020.pdf

[117] Covid lockdown related savings mean that some groups, the richer ones, have managed to pay down debt levels but for many poorer demographics debt has increased.

[118] According to debt advice provider Money Advice Service

[119] Conducted by Isabelle Guérin & Christophe Nordman & Elena Reboul, 2019. "The gender of debt and the financialisation of development. Insights from rural southern India," Working Papers CEB 19-016, ULB -- Universite Libre de Bruxelles, using Indian data disaggregated by sex, analyses the gender of debt, at the prism of caste and poverty.

[120] A job site for the over 50s, based on official figures

[121] In 2008 there were 1109 women over 65 in insolvency compared to 2082 in 2018.

[122] Household debt, austerity and gender Briefing from the UK Women's Budget Group on rising household debt levels, austerity and gender

[123] Angela Littwin, Escaping Battered Credit: A Proposal for Repairing Credit Reports Damaged by Domestic Violence, 161 U. PA. L. REv. 363, 363-80 (2013) (explaining how abused women may become subject to coerced debt)

[124] One fascinating collation of research is the 2014 report: Females on the Fringe: Considering Gender in Payday Lending Policy Amy J. Schmitz University of Missouri School of Law

[125] Nathalie Martin & Ernesto Longa, High-Interest Loans and Class: Do Payday and Title Loans Really Serve the Middle Class?, 24 LOY. CONSUMER L. REV. 524, 534-35, 534 n.44 (2012) (discussing the study)

[126] Donald P. Morgan & Kevin J. Pan, Do Payday Lenders Target Minorities?, LIBERTY STREET ECON. (Feb. 8, 2012), http://libertystreeteconomics.newyorkfed.org/2012/02/do-payday-lenders-targetminorities.html (finding that users of payday loans are worse off economically than non-users)

[127] https://www.fca.org.uk/data/consumer-credit-high-cost-short-term-credit-lending-data-jan-2019

[128] Ruth Lythe, How Women Are Being Seduced into Debt by Payday Parasites: 'Instant' Cash Firms with Interest Rates as High as 16,000% are Ruining Lives, *Daily Mail*, (Jan. 31, 2012), www.dailymail.co.uk/news/article-2094115/Instant-money-loans-Payday-loan-firms-ruininglives.html (describing advertisements airing during TV shows targeting women and payday loan websites showing young women using payday loans to make them "glamorous").

[129] See my earlier book, *10 Things Everyone Needs to Know About Money,* for a full explanation of this

[130] The rate you are offered will depend on your specific circumstances. Lenders advertise representative rates but they are only obliged to offer that to 51% of their borrowers – if they think you're particularly high-risk, they will charge you a higher rate. Strange that. Why not 290%, or 280%, and why do so many of them clustered around and quote 292%? The answer: for the simple reason that the Financial Conduct Authority has intervened in attempt to control the wilder excesses of payday loans. They have capped payday loan interest at 0.8% per day, *which equates to exactly 292% per annum!*

[131] *Financial Literacy and high-cost borrowing in the United States*, Working Paper 18969 by Annamaria Lusardi and Carlo de Bassa Scheresberg. National Bureau of Economic Research, 2013. https://www.nber.org/system/files/working_papers/w18969/w18969.pdf

[132] *Swimming with sharks: tackling illegal money lending in England.* The Centre for Social Justice, 2022. https://www.centreforsocialjustice.org.uk/wp-content/uploads/2022/03/CSJ-Illegal-lending-paper.pdf

[133] In England, Henry VIII ended the centuries-old prohibition on usury - which was then defined as lending money at any rate of interest (he capped it at 10%, thereby making lending at high rates of interest easier).

[134] As we saw with the Mexican strawberry picker and the 10 million other U.S homeowners who were lent money they would never be able to repay.

[135] *Creditocracy* is a term coined by Andrew Ross in his book of the same name. He defines it as governance or the holding of power in the interests of a creditor class and a society where access to vital needs is financed through debt. He suggested it occurs where the finance industry has commandeered elected governments forcing citizens to borrow money in order to survive. He suggests we are living in the grip of a creditocracy in many parts of the world.

[136] Rivlin, Gary. *Broke, USA: From pawnshops to Poverty, Inc.: how the working poor became big business*. Harper, 2010

[137] Published in 2010 so this figure is likely to be higher now

[138] According to a report by the American Civil Liberties Union https://www.aclu.org/issues/smart-justice/mass-incarceration/criminalization-private-debt

[139] *Debt: young women facing constant financial struggle*. Young Women's Trust, 26 November 2020. https://www.youngwomenstrust.org/our-research/debt-young-women-facing-constant-financial-struggle/

[140] https://digitalrepository.unm.edu/law_facultyscholarship/202/

[141] https://www.moneyandmentalhealth.org/wp-content/uploads/2018/12/A-Silent-Killer-Report.pdf

[142] Under federal not state law

[143] The Supreme Court ruled in 1983 that you can jail people who "wilfully refuse to pay" their debts.

[144] Why does the US still have 'debtors' prisons? BBC News, 30 April 2018 https://www.bbc.co.uk/news/av/world-us-canada-43916040 The article includes a link to the video of the news report.

[145] 2018 Report by The Institute for policy studies in the United States: https://ips-dc.org/women-racial-wealth-divide/

[146] In the video of the BBC news report mentioned earlier

[147] According to Forbers Advisor in 2021 the number of credit card users in the United States reached 196 million. "In Q4 2021, credit card users reached a total of 196 million." *9 Interesting Credit Card Statistics*, Forbes Advisor, 8 June 2022. https://www.forbes.com/advisor/credit-cards/credit-card-statistics/

[148] Another 31.6% of credit card users are *transactors* - they *don't* carry a balance so pay no financing charges. The remaining 23.8% of credit card users show no activity.

[149] FCA publishes review into unsecured credit market, 2 February 2021. https://www.fca.org.uk/news/press-releases/fca-publishes-woolard-review-unsecured-credit-market

[150] https://www.federalreserve.gov/publications/files/scf20.pdf Changes in U.S. Family Finances from 2016 to 2019: Evidence from the Survey of Consumer Finances, Federal Reserve Bulletin, September 2020. Table 2. Family median and mean net worth, by selected characteristics of families.

[151] https://www.realhomes.com/news/real-homes-reports-single-women-excluded-from-home-ownership

[152] https://wbg.org.uk/analysis/a-home-of-her-own-housing-and-women/

[153] Says Fowler, speaking at the launch of the report. Report Launch: A Home of Her Own. Smallwood Trust, 19 July 2019. https://www.smallwoodtrust.org.uk/news/report-launch-home-her-own

[154] https://hoa.org.uk/2019/03/four-reasons-your-gender-is-stopping-you-buying-a-house/

[155] Gender pay gap in U.S. held steady in 2020, Pew Research Center, 2021. https://www.pewresearch.org/fact-tank/2021/05/25/gender-pay-gap-facts/ "The gender gap in pay has remained relatively stable in the United States over the past 15 years or so. In 2020, women earned 84% of what men earned, according to a Pew Research Center analysis of median hourly earnings of both full- and part-time

workers. Based on this estimate, it would take an extra 42 days of work for women to earn what men did in 2020."

[156] Women Home Buyers, National Association of Realtors, 2021. https://www.nar.realtor/women-home-buyers "The share of single females rose slightly to 19 percent, and single males held steady at nine percent the past three years."

[157] Consumer-lending Discrimination in the FinTech Era," https://www.nber.org/papers/w25943 "Discrimination is definitely falling, and it corresponds to the rise in competition between fintech lenders and regular lenders," says Nancy Wallace, chair in real estate capital markets at Berkeley's Haas School of Business. A report by Dr. Wallace co-authored in 2019 found that fintech algorithms discriminated 40 percent less on average than face-to-face lenders in loan pricing and did not discriminate at all in accepting and rejecting loans.

[158] Overall the company reports a 532% increase in Hispanic borrowers in the 30-to-40 age range last year and a 411% increase in black borrowers.

[159] According to the National Association of Realtors. (Only 9% of home sales last year came from single males).

[160] See Carol Necole Brown, Women and Subprime Lending: An Essay Advocating SelfRegulation of the Mortgage Lending Industry, 43 IND. L. REv. 1217, 1217-22 (2010) (compiling and citing research regarding discriminatory lending). The article poses the question: "Why would people who could qualify for prime mortgage loans end up with subprime loans?" Id. at 1217.

[161] A report by the Consumer Federation of America published in 2006 notes: "Women are more likely to receive subprime mortgages than men - About a third (32.0 percent) of women borrowers receive subprime mortgage loans of all types compared to about a quarter (24.2 percent) of male borrowers."

[162] Published by the University of Chicago

[163] Cheng, Lin and Liu, 2011.

[164] Dymski, Hernandez and Mohanty 2013.

[165] The Center for Public Integrity states that this definition of predatory lending comes from a 2000 joint report from the U.S. Department of Housing and Urban Development and the Treasury Department. https://publicintegrity.org/inequality-poverty-opportunity/the-financial-meltdown-a-glossary/

[166] Student Loan Statistics by Paul Bolton. House of Commons Library, 2 December 2022. https://researchbriefings.files.parliament.uk/documents/SN01079/SN01079.pdf "Currently almost £20 billion is loaned to around 1.5 million higher education students in England each year. The value of outstanding loans at the end of March 2022 reached £182 billion. The Government forecasts the value of outstanding loans to reach around £460 billion (2021-22 prices) by the mid- 2040s. The forecast average debt among the cohort of borrowers who started their course in 2021/22 was £45,800 when they complete their course. This is expected to be lower for those starting in the reformed system from 2023/24 at £43,400. The Government expected that around 20% of full-time undergraduates starting in 2021/22 would repay them in full. They forecast that

after the 2022 reforms this would increase to 55% among new students from 2023/24."

[167] For the loans taken out more recently

[168] RPI not CPI. The Office of National Statistics has stated that the Retail Price Index is a flawed, outdated measure of inflation and states that its own official measure is Consumer Price Index. Note that CPI is consistently about 1% lower than RPI so the base interest rate that student loans are calculated from is higher than it should be.

[169] According to the House of Commons Library and the UK government.

[170] According to research by the British Household Panel Survey

[171] According to Save the Student

[172] Young Women and Student Loan Repayments, 2019 Unison National Women's Conference https://www.unison.org.uk/motions/2019/women-members/young-women-and-student-loan-repayments/

[173] Alexandria Ocasio-Cortez https://www.stylist.co.uk/people/aoc-student-loan-debt-payment-balance-alexandria-ocasio-cortez/297973

[174] Student Debt: Quick Facts, American Association of University Women, January 2022. https://www.aauw.org/app/uploads/2022/01/Student-Debt-Quick-Facts-Jan-2022.pdf

[175] Updated AAUW report, 2021 https://www.aauw.org/resources/research/deeper-in-debt/

[176] Data from student loan hero by lending tree, January 27 2021. Prior to the pandemic (defaults have been suspended at the time of writing as part of pandemic relief measures), 11.1% of student loans were delinquent by 90 days or more or were in default. But default does not mean that borrowers can walk away from their debts. If borrowers do default, the US government carves out about 15% of their post-tax income. And the loan doesn't go away. It remains outstanding. Any future income including social security income or federal subsidies to support the elderly on low incomes, can be annexed in what is an especially punitive system.

[177] *Female Start-Up founders missing out on billions in funding*. British Business Bank, 4 February 2019. https://www.british-business-bank.co.uk/press-release/female-start-up-founders-missing-out-on-billions-in-funding/

[178] Investing in Women Code: annual report. British Business Bank, 2022. https://www.british-business-bank.co.uk/wp-content/uploads/2022/06/investing-in-women-code-annual-report-2022.pdf

[179] The Alison Rose Review of Female Entrepreneurship. HM Treasury, 8 March 2019. https://www.gov.uk/government/publications/the-alison-rose-review-of-female-entrepreneurship

[180] https://www.diversity.vc/women-in-uk-vc/

[181] https://about.americanexpress.com/newsroom/press-releases/news-details/2019/Woman-Owned-Businesses-Are-Growing-2X-Faster-On-Average-Than-All-Businesses-Nationwide-09-23-2019

[182] About twice as many women as men said they started a small business during the pandemic, according to a report from Palo Alto-based Next Insurance.

[183] *Women-Led Startups Received Just 2.3% of VC Funding in 2020* by Ashley Bittner and Brigette Lau, Harvard Business Review, 25 February 2021. https://hbr.org/2021/02/women-led-startups-received-just-2-3-of-vc-funding-in-2020

[184]More women are top VC decision-makers, but parity is a long way off, Axios, 21 July 2020. https://www.axios.com/2020/07/21/women-venture-capital-gender-equality

[185] Startups With At Least 1 Female Founder Hire 2.5x More Women, Kauffman Fellows, 17 October 2019. https://www.kauffmanfellows.org/journal_posts/female_founders_hire_more_women

[186] Why Women-Owned Startups Are a Better Bet Boston Consulting Group, 6 June 2018 https://www.bcg.com/publications/2018/why-women-owned-startups-are-better-bet

[187] The report notes: "The findings are statistically significant, and we ruled out factors that could have affected investment amounts, such as education levels of the entrepreneurs and the quality of their pitches."

[188] First Round 10 Year Project http://10years.firstround.com/

[189] Research from compare the market.com published on 20 May 2020

[190] The Woolard Review into the unsecured credit market, 2022. https://www.fca.org.uk/news/press-releases/fca-publishes-woolard-review-unsecured-credit-market

[191] Consumer Credit Act. Which? Updated: 2 Jul 2021. https://www.which.co.uk/consumer-rights/regulation/consumer-credit-act-ayvHZ8H0jVl8

[192] Generation Z turning to buy now pay later schemes to fund spending during lockdown. Compare the Market, 2 June 2020. https://www.comparethemarket.com/media-centre/news/generation-z-turning-to-buy-now-pay-later-schemes-to-fund-spending-during-lockdown/

[193] The Workplace Wellbeing Study. Hastee, 2019 https://www.hasteepay.com/wp-content/uploads/2019/07/HP-workplace-wellbeing-study-2019web-FINAL.pdf

[194] One in 10 Buy Now Pay Later shoppers have been chased by debt collectors. Citizens Advice, 3 September 2021 https://www.citizensadvice.org.uk/about-us/about-us1/media/press-releases/one-in-10-buy-now-pay-later-shoppers-have-been-chased-by-debt-collectors/

[195] The Woolard Review into the unsecured credit market, 2022 (see note 190 above).

[196] According to research by CompareTheMarket.com

[197] Financial education needed after Buy Now Pay Later clampdown. Payplan, 3 February 2021. https://www.payplan.com/blog/buy-now-pay-later-clampdown

[198] The Woolard Review into the unsecured credit market, 2022 (see note 190 above).

[199] A survey released by Cardiff - a data firm that tracks consumer spending - shows that nearly half of consumers said they spend anywhere from 10% to 40% more when

they use a BNPL plan versus when the use a credit card. *Buy Now, Pay Later Credit: User Characteristics and Effects on Spending Patterns*, Marco Di Maggio, Emily Williams & Justin Katz. NBER Working Paper 30508, September 2022. https://www.nber.org/search?page=1&perPage=50&q=BNPL

[200] Quoted in *The Times*

[201] Regulation of Buy-Now Pay-Later: consultation on draft legislation. HM Treasury, 14 February 2023. https://www.gov.uk/government/consultations/regulation-of-buy-now-pay-later-consultation-on-draft-legislation

[202] Taken from a 2011 study published in the Journal of consumer psychology "if money doesn't make you happy, then you probably aren't spending it right" by Elizabeth W Dunn, Daniel T Gilbert and Timothy D Wilson. The study showed 57% of participants reported gaining greatest happiness from experiential purchases compared to 34% from material goods.

[203] As we saw above with Anne Boden's *Make Money Equal* campaigns.

[204] According to Goldman Sachs analysing data over the past 140 years in the UK.

[205] Ann's story is shared by Mind, a charity that helps people with mental health problems and campaigns to improve services, raise awareness and promote understanding. https://www.mind.org.uk/information-support/your-stories/spending-money-for-comfort/

[206] UN launches drive to highlight environmental cost of staying fashionable, 25 March 2019. https://news.un.org/en/story/2019/03/1035161

[207] How Much Do Our Wardrobes Cost to the Environment? World Bank, 23 September 2019. https://www.worldbank.org/en/news/feature/2019/09/23/costo-moda-medio-ambiente

[208] Style that's sustainable: A new fast-fashion formula, McKinsey Sustainability, 20 October 2018. https://www.mckinsey.com/capabilities/sustainability/our-insights/style-thats-sustainable-a-new-fast-fashion-formula

[209] Published by the Walk Free Foundation, walkfree.org

[210] 3.6 billion items of clothing we just don't wear. Oxfam, 6 June 2016 http://oxfamapps.org/media/hc349

[211] *Sienna Miller Launches Oxfam's #Secondhandseptember To Fight Throwaway Fashion*, 31 Aug 2021 https://www.oxfam.org.uk/media/press-releases/sienna-miller-launches-oxfams-secondhandseptember-to-fight-throwaway-fashion/

[212] According to a 2018 United Nations report

[213] In 2018 the UK exported £419 million worth of clothing overseas, the second largest exporter of clothes after the United States which exported £521 million worth. When you realise that clothing dealers pay the charities about 45 pence per kilo, the mountainous scale of the problem becomes evident.

[214] Liz Ricketts is a fashion designer, educator and founder of The Or Foundation. Her work looks at overconsumption and overproduction within the fashion industry, and attempts to engage people in alternatives. In 2011, with her partner Branson Skinner, she founded The Or Foundation, which aims to liberate young people from their

dominant consumer relationship with fashion, in an industry they describe as "riddled with excess and exploitation."

[215] 2011 article in the Journal of Consumer Psychology by Elizabeth W Dunn, Timothy D Wilson and Daniel T Gilbert

[216] https://www.vouchercodes.co.uk/savings-guides/guides-reports/personal-finance-report-2023#the-rise-of-personal-finance-gurus

[217] M. Kan and H. Laurie using British Household Panel Survey data (2010) Savings, investments, debts and psychological well-being in married and cohabiting couples https://www.iser.essex.ac.uk/research/publications/publication-514061

[218] The study by Westway and McKay in 2007 used the British Household Panel Survey (BHPS) to examine savings and investments separately for women and men. Westway, J. and McKay, S. *Women's financial assets and debts*, Fawcett Society, 2007 https://www.fawcettsociety.org.uk/Handlers/Download.ashx?IDMF=7bb3f5e4-a2f5-4758-8e08-0c04421e361a

[219] Amount of money saved in saving accounts in the United States 2019, by gender. Published by Statista Research Department, 8 February, 2023 https://www.statista.com/statistics/497799/amount-of-money-saved-in-saving-accounts-usa-by-gender/

[220] *The Role of Self-Regulation, Future Orientation, and Financial Knowledge in Long-Term Financial Decisions* by Elizabeth Howlett, Jeremy Kees, Elyria Kemp, The Journal of Consumer Affairs; Summer vol. 42, no. 2, 2008, p.223 - 242. https://doi.org/10.1111/j.1745-6606.2008.0010

[221] Credit Karma/Qualtrics survey - https://www.creditkarma.com/insights/i/one-in-three-women-discouraged-finances-survey

[222] *Religion, sex and politics? The M word is Britain's biggest taboo*. Lloyds Bank, 7 March 2019. https://www.lloydsbankinggroup.com/media/press-releases/2019/lloyds-bank/the-m-word-is-britains-biggest-taboo.html

[223] *Habit Formation and Learning in Young Children* by David Whitebread and Dr. Sue Bingham, Money Advice Service, 2013. https://maps.org.uk/wp-content/uploads/2021/03/mas-habit-formation-and-learning-in-young-children-executive-summary.pdf

[224] Named by behavioural economists Amos Tverski and Daniel Kahneman. Kahneman, Daniel, Jack L. Knetsch, and Richard H. Thaler. 1991. *Anomalies: The Endowment Effect, Loss Aversion, and Status Quo Bias*. Journal of Economic Perspectives, vol. 5 no.1, p 193-206. https://doi.org/10.1257/jep.5.1.193

[225] Thaler, Richard H., Benartzi, Shlomo. *Save More Tomorrow™: Using Behavioural Economics to Increase Employee Saving*. Journal of Political Economy vol. 112, no. S1, S164-S187. https://www.jstor.org/stable/10.1086/380085

[226] Lewis, Neil A. and Oyserman, Daphna. *When Does the Future Begin? Time Metrics Matter, Connecting Present and Future Selves*. Psychological Science vol 26, no. 6, 2015 https://doi.org/10.1177/0956797615572231

[227] *What you need to know about willpower: The psychological science of self-control*, American Psychological Association https://www.apa.org/topics/personality/willpower

[228] By Hargreaves Lansdown

[229] Branthwaite, A. and P Cooper, P., *Analgesic effects of branding in treatment of headaches*. British Medical Journal (Clin Res Ed) vol 282, no. 6276, 1985 https://doi/10.1136/bmj.282.6276.1576

[230] According to market research firm Kantar TNS as of 2018

[231] According to market research firm Kantar TNS as of 2018 *Gender investment gap estimated at £15bn Winning Over Wealth: understanding financial engagement for women* https://www.kantar.com/inspiration/finance/winning-over-wealth More detail: FT Adviser, 7 December 2018 https://www.ftadviser.com/investments/2018/12/07/gender-investment-gap-estimated-at-15bn/

[232] https://www.moneymagpie.com/manage-your-money/why-women-should-invest-in-stocks-and-shares-isas

[233] Women outpace men in signing up to investment platforms, Financial Times,1 December 2020. https://www.ft.com/content/36d9d064-d259-4d45-a637-fe2114c630e1

[234] As Ann M Carlos and Larry Neal point out in their article: *Women investors in early Capital markets 1720 to 1725* Carlos, Ann M. and Neal, Larry, Financial History Review vo. 11, no 2, 2004 , p. 197 - 224. They note: "Using a novel dataset of almost 500,000 shareholders in some of the largest British railways, we find that women were much more likely to be solo shareholders than men. There is also evidence that they prioritised their independence above other considerations such as where they invested or how diversified they could be." https://doi.org/10.1017/S0968565004000137

[235] Macdonald, W.D. *Fraud on the widow's share*, Ann Arbor: University of Michigan Law School, 1960

[236] Are women better investors than men? 28 June 2018 https://www.wbs.ac.uk/news/are-women-better-investors-than-men/

[237] Do women make better investors? Hargreaves Lansdown, 29 January 2018 https://www.hl.co.uk/news/articles/archive/do-women-make-better-investors

[238] 2021 Women and Investing Study. Fidelity Investments. https://www.fidelity.com/bin-public/060_www_fidelity_com/documents/about-fidelity/FidelityInvestmentsWomen&InvestingStudy2021.pdf

[239] The citation is of the printed version but the full text (not just the abstract) of an earlier version of the paper can be downloaded from this link. https://papers.ssrn.com/sol3/papers.cfm?abstract_id=13941

[240] *The real Wonder Women are the ones who don't take too many risks with their money*, The Times, 27 December 2020. https://www.thetimes.co.uk/article/kate-palmer-the-real-wonder-women-are-the-ones-who-dont-take-too-many-risks-with-their-money-5sdwqgx9q

[241] Compiled by researchers from Cambridge University and the London Business School, this report also shows that from 1900 to 2017 the inflation-adjusted (real

return) return on equities was positive in each location analysed, ranging typically between 3% and 6% per annum.

[242] Stripping out inflation by 6.6% every year.

[243] Stripping out inflation 5.4% per year.

[244] That's not adjusting for the effects of inflation or charges.

[245] According to research by investment firm Schroders.

[246] £1,919,261

[247] Compiled by researchers from Cambridge University and the London Business School, this report also shows that from 1900 to 2017 the inflation-adjusted (real return) return on equities was positive in each location analysed, ranging typically between 3% and 6% per annum.

[248] Stripping out inflation by 6.6% every year.

[249] Stripping out inflation 5.4% per year.

[250] There are structural problems with them however especially when more than 50% of the market invested funds - see my earlier book 10 *Things Everyone Needs to Know about Money* for more information

[251] Housel, Morgan: *The psychology of money: timeless lessons on wealth, greed, and happiness*. Harriman House, 2020

[252] The Wealth Report 2019, Knight Frank, page 73. https://content.knightfrank.com/resources/knightfrank.com.my/pdfs/the-wealth-report-2019.pdf

[253] Knight Frank report

[254] Renneboog, Luc and Spaenjers, Christophe, Hard Assets: *The Returns on Rare Diamonds and Gems*, Finance Research Letters, Vol. 9, No. 4, 2012, https://ssrn.com/abstract=1845446

[255] Lehmann, Richard *Survey of stamp values & trends*. Forbes, 5 March 2018. https://www.forbes.com/sites/richardlehmann/2018/03/05/survey-of-stamp-values-trends/

[256] https://www.maps.org.uk/2020/11/09/21-million-money-scrts-kept-from-loved-ones-across-the-uk/

[257] The cost of financial abuse in Australia: a report by Deloitte Access Economics for the Commonwealth Bank of Australia, 2022. https://www.commbank.com.au/content/dam/caas/newsroom/docs/Cost%20of%20financial%20abuse%20in%20Australia.pdf

[258] The Co-operative Bank and Refuge: Know Economic Abuse, 2020 Report by Ellie Butt, September 2020. https://www.opinium.com/wp-content/uploads/2020/10/know-economic-abuse-report.pdf

[259] The Hidden Face of Financial Abuse by Lisa Rabasca Roepe, Institute for Women's Policy Research, 20 December 2016. https://iwpr.org/media/press-hits/hidden-face-financial-abuse/

[260] Know economic abuse. The Co-operative Bank and Refuge, 2020. https://www.co-operativebank.co.uk/assets/pdf/bank/aboutus/ethicalpolicy/financialabuse/know-economic-abuse-report.pdf

[261] Finding Courage and Hope: Financial Support for Women Experiencing Domestic Violence https://www.moneygeek.com/financial-planning/resources/financial-help-women-abusive-relationships/

[262] Domestic abuse survivors have lost over £7 billion as perpetrators intercept their post, Citizens Advice warns. 28 February 2020. https://www.co-operativebank.co.uk/assets/pdf/bank/aboutus/ethicalpolicy/financialabuse/know-economic-abuse-report.pdf

[263] https://www.refuge.org.uk/wp-content/uploads/2020/10/Know-Economic-Abuse-Report-2020.pdf

[264] *Measuring the Effects of Domestic Violence on Women's Financial Well- Being* by Adrienne E. Adams, Center for Financial Security Research Brief 2011-5.6. https://centerforfinancialsecurity.files.wordpress.com/2015/04/adams2011.pdf

[265] According to *The "She-conomy" Report* by Bank of America Merrill Lynch.

[266] https://www.bcg.com/publications/2020/managing-next-decade-women-wealth

[267] *Understanding the Gender Wealth Gap, and Why It Matters* by Mark Chang, Ana Henandez Kent and Heather McCulloch. https://live-future-of-building-wealth.pantheonsite.io/wp-content/uploads/2021/09/Sec1-Ch5-Chang-Kent-McCulloch.pdf

[268] Wealth gaps between different ethnic groups in Britain are large and likely to persist. Resolution Foundation Press Release, 22 December 2020. https://www.resolutionfoundation.org/press-releases/wealth-gaps-between-different-ethnic-groups-in-britain-are-large-and-likely-to-persist/ For the full report: A gap that won't close: The distribution of wealth between ethnic groups in Great Britain by George Bangham, Resolution Foundation, December 2020. https://www.resolutionfoundation.org/app/uploads/2020/12/A-gap-that-wont-close.pdf

[269] Alyssa Schneebaum & Miriam Rehm & Katharina Mader & Katarina Hollan.The Gender Wealth Gap in Europe. WU Vienna University of Economics and Business. Department of Economics Working Paper Series No. 186, 2014. https://research.wu.ac.at/ws/portalfiles/portal/18970398/wp186.pdf

[270] Nora Waitkus & Lara Minkus (2021) Investigating the Gender Wealth Gap Across Occupational Classes, Feminist Economics, vol 27 no 4, 114-147, 2021. https://doi.org/10.1080/13545701.2021.1973059

[271] Kim Gittleson: Where are all the women in economics? BBC News, 13th of October 2017 www.bbc.co.uk/news/business-4157133

[272] Esther Duflo on the macho locker room culture of Economics, The Telegraph, 10 November 2019 https://www.telegraph.co.uk/business/2019/11/10/esther-duflo-winning-nobel-poverty-macho-locker-room-culture/

[273] macromom blog by Claudia Sahm https://macromomblog.com/2020/07/29/economics-is-a-disgrace/

Printed in Great Britain
by Amazon

24553678R00137